Health and Wealth Disparities in the United States

Health and Wealth Disparities in the United States

Anupam B. Jena
Tomas J. Philipson
Eric C. Sun

The AEI Press

Publisher for the American Enterprise Institute

WASHINGTON, D.C.

Distributed by arrangement with the Rowman & Littlefield Publishing Group, 4501 Forbes Boulevard, Suite 200, Lanham, Maryland 20706. To order, call toll free 1-800-462-6420 or 1-717-794-3800. For all other inquiries, please contact AEI Press, 1150 Seventeenth Street, N.W., Washington, D.C. 20036, or call 1-800-862-5801.

Library of Congress Cataloging-in-Publication Data

Jena, Anupam B.
    Health and wealth disparities in the United States / Anupam B. Jena,
Tomas J. Philipson, and Eric C. Sun.
        p. ; cm.
    Includes bibliographical references.
    ISBN-13: 978-0-8447-4389-9 (pbk.)
    ISBN-10: 0-8447-4389-5 (pbk.)
    ISBN-13: 978-0-8447-4390-5 (ebook)
    ISBN-10: 0-8447-4390-9 (ebook)
    1. Medical statistics—United States. 2. Income—United States—Statistics.
I. Philipson, Tomas J. II. Sun, Eric. III. Title.
    [DNLM: 1. Health Status Disparities—United States. 2. Income—United
States. WA 300 AA1]
    RA407.3.J46 2010
    614.4'273—dc22

                                                        2010025618

Printed in the United States of America

Contents

List of Illustrations

TABLES

Acknowledgments

This book extends previous work analyzing the evolution of economic disparities in an international context (Becker, Philipson, and Soares 2005). We are thankful for comments from Gary Becker, Derek Neal, Kevin Murphy, and Sam Peltzman. We appreciate financial support from the American Enterprise Institute. Anupam B. Jena and Eric C. Sun received support from the National Institutes of Health through Medical Scientist National Research Award Grant No. 5 T32 GM07281 and from the Agency for Health Care Research and Quality through UCLA/RAND Training Grant T32 HS 000046.

Introduction

Given the public interest in reducing health and income disparities, a large literature has arisen seeking to document and explain their causes and consequences. For example, with regard to income disparity in the United States, many researchers have sought to examine and explain trends in earnings disparities between blacks and whites and across education groups. Generally speaking, they have found that earnings between blacks and whites converged until the 1970s, after which the rate of convergence slowed and even reversed slightly (for a review, see Altonji and Blank 1999). Other studies have found a similar convergence in incomes across states through the 1970s, with little convergence since (see Bernat 2001 and Crain 2003). Investigations of health disparities across groups, including those defined by education, race, and gender, have also been numerous. In general, existing evidence has suggested that blacks have made consistent gains in health relative to whites since the 1970s. Interestingly, while geographic disparities in health care utilization and outcomes have been documented extensively, little effort has been made to examine how they have changed over time.

As an outgrowth of this large literature, researchers and policymakers often debate the lack of convergence in incomes across groups. This focus may not, however, lead to an understanding of true convergence in well-being, whereby individual welfare is determined not only by the income available for consumption, but by the health and length of life of the individual. A richer individual who is bedridden may be worse off than a perfectly healthy poor person. Put differently, both health *and* wealth matter for well-being. Therefore, even if yearly incomes have not converged, well-being more generally may be converging if minorities and poorer populations have seen larger than average improvements in health.

1

In this study, we formally incorporate the effect of health on well-being into an analysis of economic disparities in the United States. Traditional measures of income disparities assume that people value only material well-being, so making two groups equal is a simple matter of equating their monetary incomes. In contrast to this method, we use the economic concept of equalizing "full" income; that is, we ask how much monetary incomes would need to be changed to equate two groups, taking into account disparities in both monetary income and health. For example, if whites earned twice as much as blacks, traditional arguments would state that the two groups could be made equally well off by doubling black incomes. If whites were also much healthier than blacks, however, doubling blacks' incomes would not be sufficient to equate the two groups, since whites would remain better off even with equal incomes. Using established economic methods to value health improvements, our analysis assesses how much black incomes would need to be adjusted to equate the two groups, given differences in both income *and* health. We then compare trends in traditional income disparities over time to trends in full income disparities.

Our results suggest that accounting for the value of gains in health dramatically affects our understanding of trends in income disparities across groups, particularly across races. In 1970, black males needed to have their *monetary* incomes raised by about 75 percent to achieve income parity with white males, an amount that fell by 19 percentage points (or about a quarter in relative terms) to 56 percent in 2000. While this was a dramatic decline, our results show an even larger absolute decline in full income differences. We find that in 1970, black males needed to have their incomes raised by 111 percent to achieve parity in well-being with white males, taking into account not only the larger incomes of whites, but also the fact that they lived longer. By 2000, this had fallen by 35 percentage points to 76 percent (about a one-third decrease in relative terms) because the longevity of blacks grew faster than that of whites. Thus, whether measured in absolute or relative terms, the decline in full income disparities was larger than the decline in traditional income disparities. In the case of black females, we find similar results: reductions in full income disparities were larger than reductions in traditional income disparities, suggesting greater convergence between blacks and whites than if income alone were used to measure differences in well-being between the two races.

We also examine such full income disparities across states, but our findings here are less determinate. For blacks, we find that reductions in full income disparities are larger than reductions in traditional income disparities in poorer states, again suggesting that accounting for health leads to larger disparity reductions than when income alone is considered. For whites, we find that taking health into account does not significantly change disparity trends in income alone across states.

Overall, however, our results suggest that accounting for health is quantitatively important for any analysis of racial and geographic differences in well-being. We found that, across races, full income disparities decreased more dramatically than income disparities, with the value of gains in health accounting for roughly the same reduction in equality as changes in income. The point is not to downplay the lack of convergence in incomes, which is important and the subject of much research, but rather to observe that alternative measures, such as full income including health, suggest a more optimistic view of trends in black-white disparities. Since consumers value health in addition to monetary income, we believe full income is a more appropriate metric of trends in well-being across races and states. Our findings are the domestic analog to the international evidence of Becker, Philipson, and Soares (2005), who have found that the lack of income convergence between rich and poor countries understates the convergence in overall well-being, as it ignores the fact that poorer countries have had larger gains in longevity.

The remainder of the book is organized as follows. Chapter 1 provides an overview of the literature on health and income inequalities across races and geographic areas. Chapter 2 then provides additional context for our work by presenting and discussing the evolution of health and income differences across races and states in the United States. Chapter 3 describes our methodology for valuing gains in health, and chapter 4 presents our results.

1

Health and Wealth
Disparities in the United States:
A Brief Overview of the Literature

We begin our analysis by providing an overview of the literature on health and income disparities across races and geographic areas. First we discuss the literature on health disparities between whites and blacks, followed by an overview of wealth disparities between the two groups. We then discuss the literature on health disparities across states and, finally, conclude with a discussion of wealth disparities across states. Because the literature in each of these topics is extensive, a detailed review is beyond the scope of our analysis; interested readers are encouraged to explore the studies to which we refer for further review.

Disparities in Health across Individuals

Health disparities between whites and minorities have been the subject of numerous studies, which we briefly recount here. By and large, these disparities have been substantial. In 1940, black males in the United States had a life expectancy at birth of 51.5 years, compared to 62.1 years for white males, a difference of 10.6 years. Over time, the differences between the two groups narrowed but did not disappear; by 2004, life expectancy at birth had increased to 69.5 years for black males and 75.7 years for white males, a difference of 6.2 years. Similarly, the gap in life expectancy at birth between black and white females in 1940 was 11.7 years, which fell to 4.5 years by 2004. Although more so in 1940 than the current decade, much of the disparity in mortality between whites and blacks has

TABLE 1-1
LIFE EXPECTANCY BY AGE, BLACK AND WHITE MALES, 2004

Life expectancy in years at age	White males	Black males	Difference
0	75.7	69.5	6.2
5	71.3	65.7	5.6
25	52.0	46.7	5.3
50	29.1	25.1	4.0
75	10.7	9.9	0.8
90	4.3	4.9	−0.6

SOURCE: Arias 2007.

been due to differences in mortality at earlier ages. In 2004, for example, the infant mortality rate for blacks was still nearly double that for whites. Moreover, as shown in table 1-1, the difference in life expectancy between blacks and whites fell with increasing age.

Disparities in health between whites and minorities naturally stem at least partly from differences in care for various diseases. For example, among those with cardiovascular disease, African Americans and Mexican Americans are less likely to receive recommended medications, such as cholesterol-lowering agents, beta blockers, or ACE inhibitors, following a myocardial infarction (Herholz et al. 1996; Barnato et al. 2005). More generally, a large body of literature demonstrates that minorities are less likely to receive appropriate therapies for myocardial infarction or coronary artery disease, even after controlling for observable measures of disease severity and patient health (for example, Brown et al. 2008 and Giles et al. 1995; for a helpful review, see Kressin and Petersen 2001). Differences in care have also been demonstrated for other diseases, such as cancer (see, for example, Breslin et al. 2009 and Terplan et al. 2009) and diabetes (for a review, see Peek et al. 2007).

The reasons behind these disparities in health outcomes have been the subject of much research. A recent report by the Institute of Medicine (IOM) (2003) provides a useful outline and review of the literature. First, disparities in health outcomes may be due to patient-level attributes, such as clinical appropriateness, treatment refusal, or patient preferences. For example, blacks may prefer different types of treatments than whites, or the clinical nature of their disease may, on average, warrant different types of treatments. Although there is evidence that minorities may refuse treatment more often than whites (Hannan et al. 1999; Ayanian et al. 1999), overall, the IOM report found that these and other patient-level factors contribute little to racial health disparities. Second, disparities may be due to attributes of the health care system and the delivery of health care, such as language barriers, geographic location of health care facilities, or changes in health care financing. Finally, biases and stereotypes of health care providers may also contribute to racial disparities. Overall, the IOM report concluded that all of these sources are likely to play a role in explaining racial health care disparities.

Disparities in health due to socioeconomic status (SES) have also been the subject of numerous studies, which we briefly summarize here (for an excellent overview, see Smith 1999). The original Whitehall studies conducted in 1967 (for a review, see Marmot et al. 1999) studied health outcomes among 18,000 British civil servants. Overall, this series of studies found that British civil servants employed in lower-status positions experienced a mortality rate three times that of those in higher-status jobs. These results were replicated in a second series of Whitehall studies conducted twenty years later (Marmot et al. 1991). In this study of more than 10,000 British civil servants, the authors found that those employed in the lowest status positions were more likely to have a history of ischemic heart disease, chronic bronchitis, and obesity than persons in the highest-status jobs. Moreover, those in the lowest-status jobs experienced a fourfold increase in mortality from all causes compared to those in the highest-status jobs. In an American context, Smith (2007) used a longitudinal survey of 35,000 individuals to find that SES, whether measured by income or wealth, was associated with negative health outcomes, although education, as opposed to financial measures, primarily affected health.

In addition to examining disparities between the rich and the poor, other studies have investigated whether the presence of income disparity itself also affects health. Using data from the 1990 U.S. Census, Lynch and others (1998) found a significant association among mortality, infant mortality, and income disparities, even after adjusting for average per-capita income, a finding echoed by Kaplan and others (1996). In an excellent review of the literature, however, Deaton (2003) found little evidence of a link between income disparity and health, arguing that prior studies were limited by difficulties in measuring income and income disparities, as well as by their omission of variables such as education.

Disparities in Wealth across Individuals

Given that it is one of the central and most studied questions in economics, a detailed review of disparities in wealth across individuals is beyond the scope of this study (for excellent reviews, see Levy 2008 and Gottschalk 1997). Briefly, income disparities between whites and blacks in the United States fell around the outbreak of World War II, began rising in the mid-1970s, and accelerated in the 1980s. Efforts to explain trends in income disparities have focused on a variety of factors. The first is trade and technology, which have shifted demand away from less-skilled workers and increased the productivity of more highly skilled workers, thereby increasing disparities between the two. The second is changes in family structure, particularly the rise of multi-income households. The third is the expansion of markets due to improved communication and transportation technologies, which allow particularly highly skilled people, such as top musicians, to command particularly high salaries.

Of special interest to economists have been observed disparities in wealth and earnings across races (for a review, see Altonji and Blank 1999). While income disparities between blacks and whites declined significantly in the 1960s and 1970s, this trend slowed and even reversed after the late 1970s (Vigdor 2006). For example, using data from the U.S. Census Bureau's Current Population Survey, a large survey of U.S. households, Altonji and Blank found that in 1979, black workers received roughly 11 percent less than white workers, after controlling for education, experience, and geographic region. In 1995, the difference between the two groups was roughly the same, with blacks earning 12 percent less than whites. One explanation for the slowdown in the convergence between black and white earnings is that factors such as trade and technology, which increased the earnings gap between high- and low-skilled workers, may also have increased the disparity between whites and blacks (Juhn, Murphy, and Pierce 1991).

More generally, efforts to explain differences between white and black earnings have focused on nondiscriminatory and discriminatory sources.

Nondiscriminatory sources include differences between blacks and whites in preferences, comparative advantage, innate abilities, and education. Several studies (O'Neill 1990; Maxwell 1994; Neal and Johnson 1996) suggest that these nondiscriminatory factors may play a large role in explaining black-white income differences. In each, the authors used performance on the Armed Forces Qualifying Test (AFQT) as a measure of ability and found that blacks and whites with similar AFQT scores tended to have similar earnings, suggesting that much of the observed difference in wages between the two groups is due to differences in ability or education.

Among discriminatory sources of black-white earnings disparities, economists have generally considered two types. The first, "taste-based" discrimination, reflects the hypothesis that employers may have preferences against hiring members of certain races. The second, statistical discrimination, refers to the hypothesis that firms may use easily observable characteristics, such as race, as proxies for more difficult-to-observe characteristics, such as ability and talent. Overall, evidence suggests that both factors play a role in explaining black-white income disparities. For example, using subjects who were selected to match on all characteristics except race to interview for jobs, Turner and others (1991) found that blacks were 5.1 percent less likely to receive a job offer in Chicago, Illinois, and 13.3 percent less likely in Washington, D.C. Altonji and Pierret (2001) found evidence of statistical discrimination by noting that, if productivity is negatively correlated with a particular race, then wages should *fall* with experience, if firms do not statistically discriminate. To see why, note that if productivity were negatively correlated with a particular race, then the firm that failed to discriminate statistically would initially overestimate a worker's productivity. Over time, as the worker's lower productivity became clearer, his or her wages should fall with experience. Using this test, Altonji and Pierret found that firms did not statistically discriminate on the basis of race, but that they did statistically discriminate on the basis of education.

Disparities in Health across States

An extensive literature has also analyzed disparities in health and wealth across the more aggregated units comprised by states. With regard to health, much of the research examining geographic disparities in health care, which we only briefly summarize here, has focused on discrepancies in utilization. Using data from Medicare claims, for example, Chandra and Skinner (2004) and Baicker and others (2005) found extensive evidence of geographic variations among procedures such as hip-fracture repair, carotid endarterectomy (a procedure used to treat atherosclerosis in the carotid arteries), and percutaneous transluminal coronary angioplasty (PCTA). These variations persisted even after controlling for differences in underlying health status across states. The authors argued that these geographic variations in practice at both the practitioner and hospital levels, coupled with the fact that minorities often seek care from different hospitals than whites, may explain some of the disparities in health outcomes across races. For example, in related work, Skinner and Zhou (2006) found that patients in wealthier areas experienced larger increases in life expectancy between 1982 and 1991 and were more likely to receive recommended treatments, such as mammograms and beta blockers, than those in poorer areas.

Despite these findings, increased utilization is not always associated with higher quality of care as perceived by patients, according to Fowler and others (2008). It is useful to note that, while research into geographic variations in health care utilization and outcomes has been extensive, less emphasis has been placed on how these geographic disparities have evolved over time. An important exception is Peltzman (2009a; 2009b), who has traced disparities in longevity across U.S. states between 1900 and 2005. Peltzman found that disparities in longevity declined sharply between 1900 and 1960 but have remained largely constant since. Peltzman also found that the trend in longevity disparities across U.S. counties between 1970 and 2000 mirrors trends in income disparities, with both decreasing between 1970 and 1980 and then increasing slightly. Moreover, Peltzman found that in the United States and abroad, historical declines in mortality disparities have been on the order of, if not larger than, declines in income disparity.

Disparities in Wealth across States

To complement the early analysis by macroeconomists of income equality and growth across countries, substantial research has been conducted into the patterns and causes of income disparities across the smaller geographic units comprised by states. First applied to international income disparities, standard neoclassical growth theory predicted that the incomes of poorer nations would converge with those of wealthier ones, though post–World War patterns in income disparities have not supported this hypothesis (see, for example, Barro and Sala-i-Martin 1995; De la Fuente 1997; Mankiw et al. 1992; Quah 1996; Parente and Prescott 1993). The assumption underlying this theory is that output in an economy is driven by three factors: labor, capital, and technology. When labor and capital are freely mobile across borders, higher returns in a region to either factor will induce migration toward that region, thereby leading to convergence. Moreover, because the neoclassical model assumes diminishing returns to both capital and labor—such that increases in output are smaller with each subsequent increase in either—convergence in income is expected to occur across countries for this reason, as well. Therefore, wealthier economies are expected to grow more slowly and poorer economies more rapidly, due to both diminishing returns and the migration of factors toward economies with higher returns.

Because the flow of labor, capital, and technology is much more easily achieved across state lines than international borders, a growing literature has analyzed the issue of income convergence across American states. Perhaps the earliest such analysis was by Barro and Sala-i-Martin (1992), who studied convergence in income per capita and gross state product per capita across the forty-eight contiguous U.S. states for the years 1840–1988. These authors found evidence of convergence in the sense that wealthier states in per-capita terms tended to grow more slowly than poorer states during the time period studied. Their analysis of ninety-eight countries revealed no such evidence of convergence unless they accounted for other institutional variables, such as high school enrollment rates and the ratio of government consumption to gross domestic product—a concept referred to as conditional convergence. A related analysis of seventy-three regions in Europe—eleven in Germany, eleven in the United Kingdom, twenty in Italy, twenty-one in France, four in the Netherlands, three in Belgium, and three in Denmark—by the same authors revealed a similar pattern of convergence to that noted in their U.S. analysis (Barro and Sala-i-Martin 1991).

Since these initial analyses, several studies have more fully characterized the process of state convergence in the U.S. setting. From a time series standpoint, income convergence across states seems to have been most rapid until the late 1970s, at which point no further convergence occurred (Bernat 2001; Crain 2003). While several explanations are possible, some light may be shed on this phenomenon by alternative models of growth that emphasize increasing returns to physical and/or human capital, which may lead to divergence as certain states accumulate more of one or the other; see, for example, Romer (1986) or Lucas (1988).

Multiple studies, including one of the initial ones by Barro and Sala-i-Martin (1991), have also analyzed the sources of convergence across U.S. states. In particular, because both income and gross state product per capita depend on the composition of employment sectors in a state, a natural question they have addressed is how specific sectors have converged across states. For example, for the period 1963–89, Barro and Sala-i-Martin (1991) found convergence for all sectors across states. In a follow-up analysis, Bernard and Jones (1996) obtained slightly different results—namely, that convergence in the manufacturing sector across states was mainly responsible for state-level convergence in income during the same time period (see also Kim 1998 for a related analysis). Construction and retail industries showed no evidence of convergence. Put together, increases in within-sector productivity accounted for nearly three-quarters of the convergence in income across states in the Bernard and Jones study, with changes in the sectoral composition of states accounting for the remainder.

Conclusions

Overall, our review of the literature on racial and geographic disparities in health and wealth suggests the following:

- Although racial disparities in health continue to exist between blacks and whites, the gap between the two races has narrowed sharply since 1940.

- The gap between black and white wages narrowed sharply in the 1960s and 1970s but has stayed roughly constant and even widened slightly since then.

- Convergence in income across states was most rapid until the late 1970s but has since remained constant.

- Wide disparities remain across geographic regions in health outcomes and utilization, although little work has examined their course over time.

In sum, it appears that across races and states, little reduction in income disparity has taken place since the late 1970s. While the literature suggests that large reductions in racial health disparities have occurred since the 1970s, it is largely silent on movements in health disparities across states during this time frame. In this context, the goal of our study is to examine the degree to which considering income and health disparities in isolation may lead us to misstate the evolution of disparities in economic well-being, a measure that incorporates changes in both health *and* wealth. For example, even if the gap between white and black earnings has remained constant since the 1970s, this lack of movement may understate true gains in the relative well-being of blacks and whites if blacks made tremendous relative advances in health. Given that the literature has generally found little movement in income disparities across races and states since the late 1970s, our goal is to determine the extent to which potential reductions in health disparities over this time period have reduced disparities in overall well-being.

2

Historical Evolution of Health and Wealth Disparities

In the previous chapter, we reviewed the vast literature on racial and geographic disparities in health and wealth in the United States. In this chapter, we provide some context for these disparities by describing the evolution over time of health and wealth disparities between races and among states.

Evolution of Health by Race

This section and the next characterize the aggregate evolution of health and wealth disparities between American blacks and whites from 1970 to 2000. While much research effort has been devoted to understanding the determinants of these disparities, little emphasis has been placed on how improvements in health have affected our understanding of the evolution of economic disparities between the two groups.

Measuring health is difficult. Improvements in health may generally be divided into extensions in the quantity of life and the quality of those additional months or years one lives. Importantly, while a complete measure of health would ideally incorporate both the quantity and quality of life, our main measure focuses only on the former. In particular, we address the evolution of health by focusing our attention on changes in lifetime survival at birth.

Lifetime survival curves tell us how likely an individual is to make it to each successive year of life after birth, and, as one might expect, this is directly related to the average life expectancy at birth. Such survival curves can generally be computed in one of two ways. The first, often called the

FIGURE 2-1

LIFE EXPECTANCY BY RACE AND GENDER, 1940–2000

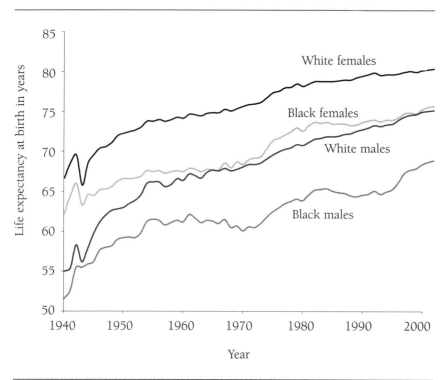

SOURCE: Arias 2007.

cohort-based approach, follows a sample of individuals over time and cal-
culates the fraction who die at each subsequent year after birth. In the context of our analysis, the natural problem with this approach is that one
would have to follow individuals for many years, an obvious limitation if
one is trying to compute survival prospects in the year 2000. The preferred
method, typically referred to as the period-based approach, allows for the
computation of lifetime survival curves in any period. For instance, the lifetime probability of a sixty-year-old's surviving from this year to the next is
determined by the fraction of sixty-year-olds alive in the year 1999 who are
not alive in 2000. Using a period-based approach, then, one can easily compare how lifetime survival—and life expectancy—at birth compare across
time periods.

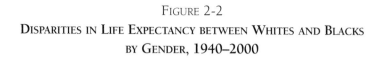

Figure 2-2

Disparities in Life Expectancy between Whites and Blacks
by Gender, 1940–2000

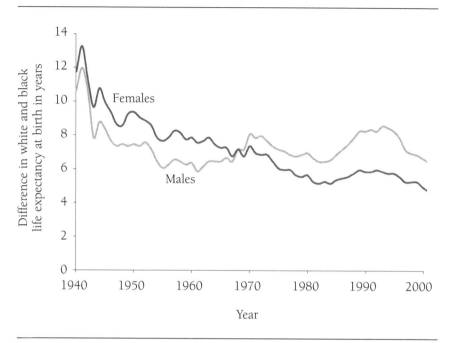

Source: Arias 2007.

Figure 2-1 shows life expectancy by race and gender between 1940 and 2000. In 1940, white males had a life expectancy of 62.1 years, compared to 51.5 years for black males, a difference of 10.6 years. By 2000, the difference had narrowed to 6.6 years, with white males having a life expectancy of 74.9 years and black males having a life expectancy of 68.3 years. Similarly, in 1940, white females had a life expectancy 11.7 years greater than their black counterparts (66.6 versus 54.9 years, respectively); by the year 2000, the gap had narrowed to 6.6 years.

To provide a broader perspective of the evolution of disparities in white and black health, figure 2-2 traces the differences in life expectancy at birth between whites and blacks by gender. As previously discussed, while white males and females continue to have higher life expectancy than their black counterparts, this difference has been falling over time. For females, the

FIGURE 2-3

WHITE SURVIVAL AT BIRTH FOR TOP AND BOTTOM QUARTILES OF U.S. STATES IN TERMS OF LIFE EXPECTANCY, 1977 AND 2000

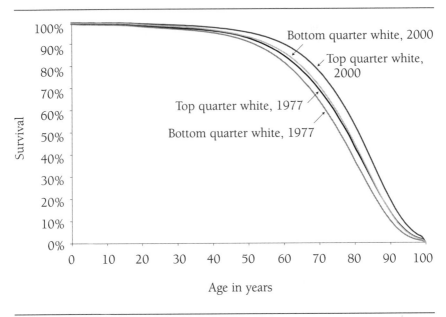

SOURCE: Authors' calculations based on mortality vital statistics data available from the National Center for Health Statistics (Arias 2007). For further details on data and methods, see chapter 3.

disparity between whites and blacks appears to have declined steadily between 1940 and 2000. Changes in the disparity between white and black males, however, have been more erratic. Between 1940 and the mid-1960s, the disparity between the two declined; it then actually increased slightly until the 1970s. Similarly, while the disparity between white and black life expectancy declined overall between 1970 and 2000, the change consisted of three phases: an initial decline between 1970 and the mid-1980s, an increase until the early 1990s, and another steady decline starting in the early 1990s.

While figures 2-1 and 2-2 demonstrate both the underlying disparity in nationwide survival between blacks and whites in the year 1970 and the partial convergence that occurred over the next thirty years, they mask the variation in life expectancy and the evolution of that variation within each

FIGURE 2-4

**BLACK SURVIVAL AT BIRTH FOR TOP AND BOTTOM QUARTILES
OF U.S. STATES IN TERMS OF LIFE EXPECTANCY, 1977 AND 2000**

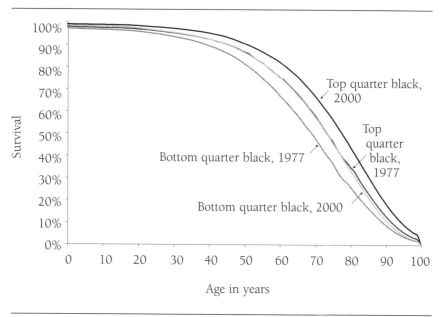

SOURCE: Authors' calculations based on mortality vital statistics data available from the National Center for Health Statistics (Arias 2007). For further details on data and methods, see chapter 3.

group. To analyze this further, figure 2-3 shows the average survival curves at birth for whites in 1977 and 2000 for the bottom and top quartiles of states in terms of white life expectancy. Similarly, figure 2-4 displays the average survival at birth for blacks in the bottom and top quartiles of states for 1977 and 2000. We use 1977 as our baseline year, since state-specific survival data are not available for all fifty states prior to that point.

Figure 2-3 shows that in 1977, whites in the bottom quartile of states in terms of life expectancy had slightly lower survival prospects than those in the top quartile. Specifically, whites in states in the top quartile of white life expectancy had an 82.1 percent chance of living to age sixty, compared to a 77.8 percent chance in states in the bottom quartile. Life expectancy in 1977 was 72.2 and 70.0 years in the top and bottom quartiles of states, respectively. Compared to 1977, life expectancy grew in the top quartile of states by approximately 6.1 years (8.4 percent) and in the bottom quartile of states by 5.4 years (7.8 percent), suggesting no apparent convergence in white survival between the highest and lowest quartile of states.

An analysis of black survival at birth for the top and bottom quartiles of states in terms of life expectancy reveals a moderately different pattern. For example, figure 2-4 illustrates that in 1977, the difference in black lifetime survival at birth between the bottom and top quartiles of states was substantially greater than the disparity for whites. In the bottom quartile, blacks had a 60.3 percent chance of living to age sixty, compared to a 69.0 percent chance in the top quartile. In terms of life expectancy in 1977, this amounts to a 4.2 year difference in black life expectancy between the top and bottom quartile states (66.2 years and 62.0 years, respectively), compared to a 2.2 year difference for the comparable measure for whites. Figure 2-4 demonstrates an equivalent lack of convergence in black survival between the top and bottom quartiles of states. For example, in 2000, black life expectancy at birth in the top and bottom quartiles of states was 74.6 years and 70.0 years respectively, a difference of 4.6 years. In percentage terms, black life expectancy at birth grew 12.7 percent and 10.7 percent in the top and bottom quartiles of states, respectively, indicating that although black survival grew faster than white survival in the same twenty-three-year period, both groups witnessed little convergence in within-race disparity.

Evolution of Wealth by Race

As already discussed, economists have expended considerable effort trying to understand the basic determinants of the U.S. wage structure, as well as the key factors contributing to changes in income disparities between blacks and whites. Because we are primarily interested in the evolution of economic well-being—which comprises both income and the value of health—understanding aggregate changes in income is as important as understanding aggregate changes in health.

Figure 2-5, therefore, plots income per capita for blacks and whites from 1970 to 2000, with income measured in year 2008 dollars. In this and all subsequent analysis, income data are obtained by aggregating individual-level data collected from the joint U.S. Census Bureau and Bureau of Labor Statistics Current Population Surveys from 1970 to 2000.[1]

FIGURE 2-5

TIME SERIES OF INCOME PER CAPITA FOR BLACKS AND WHITES, 1970–2000

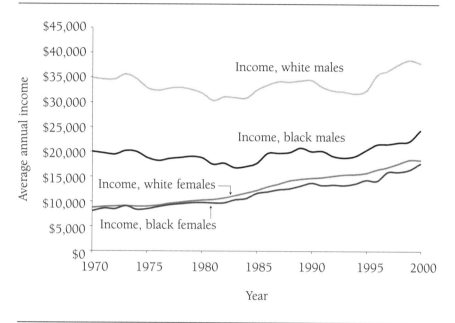

SOURCE: Authors' calculations based on data obtained from the U.S. Current Population Surveys basic monthly (March) survey (U.S. Census Bureau 2000).
NOTE: All dollar values are in 2008 dollars.

Figure 2-5 shows that, in per-capita terms, the absolute difference between white and black incomes has remained relatively constant over time for both males and females. In 1970, black males earned an average of $19,807 annually, while white males earned $34,690, a difference of $14,883. Thirty years later, black males earned $24,132 annually, compared to $37,726 among white males, a difference of $13,594. In percentage terms, however, black males earned 57 percent as much as their white counterparts in 1970, increasing to 64 percent in 2000, a natural conse-quence of both groups experiencing roughly equivalent absolute increases in income. In relative terms, then, blacks and whites experienced a moder-ate degree of convergence in per-capita income from 1970 to 2000. In con-trast to black males, black females had earnings similar to those of their white counterparts, although the absolute differences remained roughly the same over time. In 1970, black females earned $7,889, compared to $8,558 for their white counterparts, a difference of $669. Thirty years later, black females earned $17,506, an amount that was $691 less than for white females. In percentage terms, black females received 92 percent of their white counterparts' earnings in 1970 and 96 percent in 2000. Overall then, our results show little convergence in black-white incomes since the 1970s, a finding mirrored by others (Altonji and Blank 1999).

Putting together our aggregate findings on the evolution of health and wealth disparities for American blacks and whites from 1970 to 2000, we may see a preview of our later results. The partial convergence in economic disparity as measured solely by income per capita apparently should only be strengthened when the value of improvements in black longevity is incorporated into the calculation. Whether convergence will be strengthened or weakened will depend not only on the magnitude of relative improvements in survival between whites and blacks, but also on the relative value of those improvements. Because the economic value of improvements in health traditionally depends positively on income, the contribution of improvements in longevity to economic well-being will necessarily be higher for wealthier groups. The implication is that even if blacks have experienced the same or higher gains in life expectancy as whites, the economic value of those gains could be lower, given their lower income. Convergence in that case might not be strengthened by incorporating the value of improved longevity.

Evolution of Health across States

While an abundant literature analyzes the evolution of economic disparity across countries, that discussing the evolution of economic disparity across states is sizably smaller. Similarly, while most studies of health disparities have generally focused on differences in health across race, income, education, and so forth, less emphasis has been placed on the evolution of health disparities across states. As such, our primary interest is to tie these two literatures together by analyzing the impact of longevity improvements within states on the evolution of economic disparity across states.

As a graphical complement to our discussion of black-white inequalities in survival, we can analyze how survival has changed for individuals in the

FIGURE 2-6

SURVIVAL AT BIRTH FOR TOP AND BOTTOM QUARTILES OF U.S. STATES
IN TERMS OF INCOME PER CAPITA, 1977–2000

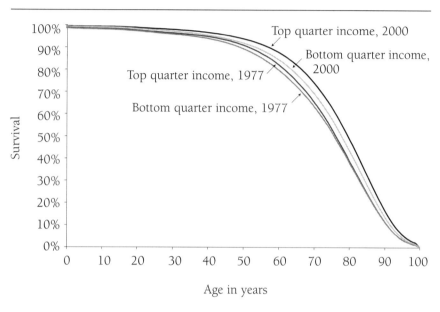

SOURCE: Authors' calculations based on mortality vital statistics data available from the National Center for Health Statistics (Arias 2007). State income data are calculated from U.S. Current Population Survey (U.S. Census Bureau 2000). For details on survival curve calculations, see chapter 3.

poorest and wealthiest U.S. states. Figure 2-6 illustrates this by showing how survival at birth differed between the top and bottom quartiles of states in terms of income per capita in 1977 and explores how this relationship had changed by the year 2000. As before, state-level income is computed from individual-level data collected from the Current Population Surveys of 1977 and 2000.

The figure illustrates several interesting patterns. First, in 1977, aggregate survival at birth differed only slightly between the wealthiest and poorest quartiles of U.S. states. For example, life expectancy in the poorest quartile was 72.1 years, compared to 73.0 years in the wealthiest quartile, a difference of only about ten months. Second, this difference grew substantially over the next two decades, with life expectancy in the poorest quartile

FIGURE 2-7

TIME SERIES OF INCOME PER CAPITA FOR TOP AND BOTTOM QUARTILES
OF U.S. STATES, 1970–2000

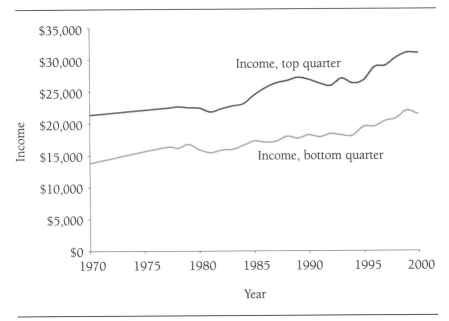

SOURCE: Income data for 1970 are drawn from the U.S. Census Public Use Microdata Samples (Ruggles et al. 2008). Income data for remaining years are drawn from the CPS (U.S. Census Bureau 2000). NOTE: There are no observations between 1970 and 1977. All dollar values are in 2008 dollars.

of states nearing 74.7 years in the year 2000, compared to 76.8 years for the wealthiest quartile. Put differently, the difference in life expectancy between the wealthiest and poorest quartiles of states more than doubled, from about ten months to 2.1 years, suggesting a divergence in health between the poorest and wealthiest states.

Evolution of Wealth across States

Alongside our analysis of the evolution of income per capita for American blacks and whites, we can also characterize the evolution of income per capita in terms of the lowest and highest quartiles of U.S. states. The intent is to examine how growth in per-capita income has varied for the richest and poorest states over time. These time series results are displayed in figure 2-7.

Contrary to our findings for American blacks and whites, figure 2-7 displays a pattern of partial divergence in income per capita for the wealthiest and poorest states. To be sure, in 1970, the average income per capita in the poorest quartile of states was $13,725 (in 2008 dollars), compared to $21,225 in the wealthiest quartile, a difference of $7,500. In 2000, the average income per capita in the poorest quartile of states was $21,274, or $9,587 lower than the income per capita of $30,861 in the wealthiest quartile. In relative terms, however, the poorest quartile of states converged toward the wealthiest quartile, as income per capita was 54.6 percent higher in the wealthiest quartile in 1977 and 45 percent higher in 2000. Unlike the trend toward wealth convergence observed between blacks and whites, wealth appears to have diverged between the wealthiest and poorest states from 1977 to 2000.

Standard Measures of Health and Wealth Disparities across States

While the previous discussion provides illustrative support for divergence in both wealth and health across states and races, we can use more formal measures—commonly employed in the cross-country growth literature—to measure differences in health and wealth across states over time. Table 2-1 presents several such measures, including the Gini coefficient, the coefficient of variation, the standard deviation of log variable of interest, and the relative mean deviation. Each measure is designed to reflect the underlying amount of dispersion present in the variable of interest, with higher values reflecting more dispersion. For example, the Gini coefficient takes on values between 0 and 1, with 1 representing full inequality and 0 representing full equality across groups. Similarly, the coefficient of variation is a dimensionless number given simply by the standard deviation of the variable of interest divided by the mean. It therefore provides a related measure of dispersion of the underlying data (for more information on these measures, please refer to Atkinson 1970).

Importantly, although these measures are typically used to describe inequality in income data, they may also describe inequality across groups for other variables—for example, life expectancy. As such, we present inequality measures for both income and life expectancy across states. For

TABLE 2-1

EVOLUTION OF HEALTH AND WEALTH DISPARITIES ACROSS U.S. STATES,
WHITES, 1940–2000

Group	Inequality measure	Life expectancy			Income per capita		
		1940	1970	2000	1940	1970	2000
Men	Gini coefficient	0.012	0.006	0.008	0.145	0.083	0.082
	Coeff. of variation	0.022	0.011	0.015	0.256	0.146	0.147
	Std. dev. of logs	0.022	0.011	0.015	0.279	0.153	0.148
	Relative mean dev.	0.008	0.004	0.006	0.111	0.062	0.060
Women	Gini coefficient	0.009	0.004	0.006	0.191	0.082	0.085
	Coeff. of variation	0.017	0.008	0.011	0.362	0.151	0.153
	Std. dev. of logs	0.017	0.008	0.011	0.349	0.152	0.152
	Relative mean dev.	0.006	0.003	0.005	0.143	0.062	0.064

SOURCE: Authors' calculations of income from the U.S. Census Public Use Microdata Samples (Ruggles et al. 2008). Data on life expectancy come from the National Center for Health Statistics (Arias 2007).

whites, available data allow us to examine trends in inequality between 1940 and 2000, while for blacks, we examine the period from 1970 to 2000. All inequality measures are weighted by state population in the relevant year.

Table 2-1 shows that for whites, income inequality across states has trended downward over the time periods examined. For white males, the Gini coefficient for income was 0.145 in 1940, and it fell by nearly half to 0.082 in 2000, consistent with trends in the other measures of inequality shown in table 2-1. Table 2-1 also suggests that for white males, income inequality across states has remained fairly constant since 1970. For white females, a similar story emerges: The Gini coefficient for income was 0.191 in 1940, fell to 0.082 in 1970, and rose slightly to 0.085 in 2000. Thus, as with their male counterparts, income inequality for white females generally decreased between 1940 and 2000 but remained steady and even increased slightly from 1970 to 2000.

For whites, trends in health inequality, as measured by the Gini coefficient for life expectancy across states, generally mirrored those for income inequality, although it is useful to note, first, that in general, inequality in income exceeded inequality in health, and, second, that health converged

TABLE 2-2

EVOLUTION OF HEALTH AND WEALTH DISPARITIES ACROSS U.S. STATES,
BLACKS, 1970–2000

Group	Inequality measure	Life expectancy 1970	Life expectancy 2000	Income per capita 1970	Income per capita 2000
Men	Gini coefficient	0.022	0.015	0.162	0.076
	Coeff. of variation	0.044	0.028	0.291	0.140
	Std. dev. of logs	0.043	0.027	0.317	0.148
	Relative mean dev.	0.016	0.010	0.134	0.054
Women	Gini coefficient	0.018	0.010	0.180	0.079
	Coeff. of variation	0.038	0.022	0.320	0.152
	Std. dev. of logs	0.038	0.021	0.348	0.152
	Relative mean dev.	0.012	0.007	0.140	0.052

SOURCE: Authors' calculations of income from the U.S. Census Public Use Microdata Samples (Ruggles et al. 2008). Data on life expectancy come from the National Center for Health Statistics (Arias 2007).

less than income. For example, for white males, the Gini coefficient for life expectancy in 1940, 0.012, was smaller than the Gini coefficient for income, and it decreased to 0.008 in 2000—a smaller decrease in both absolute and relative terms than that in income inequality over this time. Interestingly, the Gini coefficient for life expectancy was 0.006 in 1970, suggesting that health inequality has actually increased for white males since then. Similarly, for white females, the Gini coefficient for life expectancy was 0.009 in 1940, fell to 0.004 in 1970, and rose to 0.006 in 2000. In sum, for whites, income and health inequality fell drastically between 1940 and 1970, but they seem to have risen slightly since.

Similar values for blacks are shown in table 2-2, although data limitations allow us to analyze trends only between 1970 and 2000.[2] Reductions in income inequality between 1970 and 2000 were on the same order of magnitude as those observed for whites between 1940 and 1970, with the Gini coefficient falling from 0.162 to 0.076 for men and from 0.180 to 0.079 for women. Health inequality decreased as well, with the Gini coefficient for black males falling from 0.022 to 0.015 and for females from 0.018 to 0.010. Although the absolute value of these reductions was smaller than those in income inequality, the relative reduction (roughly 50 percent) was in line with the relative reductions in income inequality. Thus, in contrast to whites, income and health inequality among blacks has decreased dramatically since 1970, although the lack of data prevents us from comparing the magnitude of these changes against earlier changes in black inequality. In addition, for blacks, relative reductions in health inequality were on the same order as relative reductions in income inequality.

3

Valuing Improvements in Health

As the previous chapters discuss, understanding the evolution of economic well-being across states—or different socioeconomic groups—requires an understanding not only of how income evolves over time but also of how other nonmarket goods that increase economic well-being evolve. Of particular interest to us is a natural commodity that increases economic well-being but is not captured in standard measures of it—namely, the quantity of life. To characterize fully the evolution of economic welfare across states or between blacks and whites, it is, therefore, important to have a methodology that allows us to incorporate the value of improvements in health into changes in income profiles.

A Framework for Valuing Health Gains and Income Disparities

Our framework for evaluating disparities in well-being among groups, whether across races or across states, is based on a simple question: how much money would persons in one group need to be compensated to be as well off as persons in another group? For example, given that whites are healthier and earn more than blacks, how much would blacks need to be compensated to be as well off as whites, and how has this amount changed over time? Traditional methods of measuring disparities in well-being assume that monetary income alone reflects an individual's well-being. From this perspective, the amount needed to make blacks as well off as whites is simply the income difference between the two—for example, if blacks earn half as much as whites, traditional methods of assessing inequality would conclude that blacks could be made as well off as whites by doubling their income.

These methods, however, are likely incomplete, as individuals value other commodities besides income, such as improved health. Returning to the example above, if whites earn twice as much as blacks *and* are healthier as well, then doubling black income will equate the two groups' earnings, but *not* their total well-being, since whites are, on average, healthier than blacks. Thus, black incomes would have to be more than doubled to equate the two groups' total well-being. This concept can be conveyed by simple calculus. Suppose, for example, that an individual's utility for lifetime income (Y) and health (S) can be represented by $V(Y,S)$. Now consider two groups, one with health and income S and Y and another with better health S' and higher income Y'. The disparity between these two groups can be measured by the additional lifetime income WTA that must be provided to the first group to leave it equally well off as the second group. Functionally, WTA is the monetary amount by which the first group must be compensated to equate utility levels between the two groups:

$$V(Y + WTA, S) = V(Y', S') \qquad (1)$$

Traditional methods of valuing disparities in well-being inherently assume that utility is a function of income only, so that $V(Y,S) = V(Y)$. In this case, it is trivial to show that WTA is simply the difference in income between the two groups, so that $WTA = Y' - Y$. However, equation (1) shows that when consumers value health in addition to income, WTA no longer equals the difference in incomes between the two groups. Indeed, if health is valued by individuals (mathematically, $V_S > 0$), it is easy to show that if the wealthier group is also healthier (so that $S' > S$), then WTA will be larger than the difference in incomes, reflecting the fact that poorer individuals must be compensated for both the difference in incomes and the difference in health.[3] We refer to WTA as the amount that equalizes the *full income,* or well-being, of both groups; this amount accounts for the value of both monetary income and health.

An important point to make is that WTA, the difference in full income or well-being between two groups, will rise with income, even when health is held constant. For example, suppose that whites live twice as long as blacks, and consider two cases: one where both groups earn $10,000 per year, and one where both groups earn $20,000 per year. Even though the black-white health differential is the same in these two cases, WTA will be higher in the second case because the incomes of both groups are higher. *WTA* rises with income because higher incomes increase consumption, thereby making an additional year of life more valuable. Since *WTA* naturally rises with income, our approach will be to represent *WTA* as a share of income *Y*. In other words, we report the relative amount (that is, the percentage) by which incomes of the poorer group must be increased to equate well-being with a richer group, as opposed to the absolute amount. Reporting the relative amount allows us to account for increases in income, thereby allowing us to compare *WTA* meaningfully over periods when incomes are changing.

Our basic approach toward calculating *WTA* adopts the framework developed by Becker, Philipson, and Soares (2005), who analyzed the impact of valuing improvements in longevity on cross-country convergence in economic welfare. Similar to these authors, we value the improvement in health for a given group (whether a particular state or racial group) by considering a hypothetical individual who represents the average person in that group. For a given year and group, this hypothetical individual is assumed to face both the cross-sectional (or period) survival and income for every year of his or her life. For example, to compare disparities between white and black males in 1970, our analysis would compare two hypothetical individuals. The first faces the cross-sectional survival of an average black male in 1970 and earns 1970 black male per-capita income every year of his life. The second faces the cross-sectional survival of an average white male in 1970 and earns 1970 white male per-capita income every year of his life. We would then use equation (1) to estimate the amount black males would need to be compensated to be just as well off as white males. From equation (1), this value can be determined given (a) assumptions on the nature of the utility function $V(Y, S)$, (b) estimates of lifetime incomes *Y*, and (c) estimates of survival prospects *S*. Our methodology for determining the nature of $V(Y, S)$ follows that of Becker and others (2005) and is discussed in more detail in the appendix. Details for how we estimate incomes and survival prospects are presented in detail below.

Estimating Incomes and Health Gains

To evaluate disparities in "full income" across racial groups and across states over time, we required income and survival data over time for blacks and whites in the U.S. population as a whole and for blacks and whites across states. We used the U.S. Census Public Use Microdata Sample (Ruggles et al. 2008), a 5 percent sample of the U.S. population, to compute national per-capita incomes in the years 1940, 1970, and 2000 for blacks and whites. For our state-level analysis, we calculated state-specific estimates of income per capita for both blacks and whites for those years, as well.

For 1940 and 1970 survival data, we obtained national and state-specific life tables for blacks and whites published by the National Center of Health Statistics (Arias 2007). Importantly, published state-specific life tables for 1940 exist only for whites. Published life tables for 1970 include survival data for whites in all fifty states and for blacks in twenty-seven states. Because the National Center for Health Statistics has not yet published life tables by state, single years of age, race, or gender for year 2000 survival data, we calculated those life tables ourselves. Death certificate data, also obtained from the National Center for Health Statistics, provided a record of every death in the United States. Using them, we were able to calculate the number of deaths by race, gender, age, and state. We then linked these data with population data by race, gender, age, and state obtained from the U.S. Census and calculated life tables following procedures outlined by the National Center for Health Statistics (Arias 2007).

Fundamentally, the life table for each demographic group is calculated by estimating the probability that a person in a particular demographic group of age n dies before reaching age $n + 1$. This probability is estimated as

$$\frac{D_n}{P_n + 0.5D_n} \tag{2}$$

where D_n is the number of people in the demographic group who died at age n, and P_n is the total population of people in the given demographic group at age n. Using equation (2), we then calculated the year 2000 life tables by state, age, gender, and race.[4] With these data on incomes and survival, we can calculate the value of health gains over time.

4

Health and the Evolution
of Economic Disparities

In chapters 1 and 2, we examined the evolution of racial and geographic disparities in health and wealth in the United States. Our results suggested that accounting for the value of health gains, particularly among minorities, could have implications for understanding the overall evolution of health and wealth equality in the United States. Toward this end, chapter 3 described our methodology for estimating the value of U.S. health improvements within races and states. In this chapter, we describe our results. We begin by presenting changes in income disparity over time, measured by the disparity in monetary income between poorer and wealthier groups. We then calculate the amount by which poorer groups must be compensated to achieve parity in full income or well-being with wealthier groups, taking into account disparities in income *and* health. Finally, we examine how these two measures of well-being have changed over time.

Health and the Evolution of Economic Disparities across Races

As discussed previously, between 1970 and 2000, the absolute difference in earnings between U.S. blacks and whites remained relatively constant at around $7,000, although the relative difference between the two races fell, with blacks earning 64 percent of white earnings in 1970 and 74 percent in 2000. These commonly used measures of income disparities only take into account changes in monetary income, however. Our goal is to examine whether taking into account full income, which incorporates the monetary value of changes in health, significantly reduces the gap between blacks and whites, particularly since, as we saw in the previous chapter, gains in black health outpaced gains in white health during this time.

We begin with table 4-1, which summarizes changes in annual income for blacks and whites from 1970 to 2000. The first two columns show average annual incomes for blacks and whites. In 1970, black males earned $19,807, on average, compared to $34,690 for white males, while in 2000 black males earned $24,132, compared to $37,726 for white males. The third column in the table, "traditional income disparity," shows the percentage increase in black incomes required to achieve income parity between blacks and whites. As shown, in 1970, black males required a 75 percent increase in income to achieve parity, which fell to 56 percent in 2000—a decrease of nineteen percentage points. Similarly, black females required a 9 percent income increase to achieve parity with whites in 1970 and a 4 percent increase in 2000. Taken together, the first three columns of table 4-1 show that the black-white earnings gap narrowed between 1970 and 2000, particularly for black males, although the gap between black and white males remained large.

In contrast to the first three columns of table 4-1, which focus solely on income disparities between blacks and whites, the last two columns show black-white disparities taking health disparities into account, using the methods discussed in chapter 3. The fourth column in the table, "WTA," shows the absolute increase in black incomes required to achieve parity with whites in total economic well-being. The last column, "full income disparity," expresses this amount as a percentage of black incomes in that period. The crucial comparison, then, is between "traditional income disparity," the percentage income increase required to achieve income parity, and "full income disparity," the percentage income increase required to achieve parity in well-being.

When health is taken into account, black males in 1970 would have to be compensated by $21,916, an increase 111 percent above their 1970 income of $19,807, to achieve parity in full income with whites. This value is larger than the 75 percent increase in 1970 income required to achieve income parity alone and simply reflects the poorer survival prospects of black males compared to their white counterparts. By 2000, however, black males required a 76 percent increase in income to achieve full income parity with whites, a decrease of thirty-five percentage points (32 percent relative decline). When income alone is considered as the measure of well-being, our results suggest that the disparity between blacks and whites fell by nineteen percentage points (25 percent relative decline). Thus, in both absolute and relative terms, the disparity between blacks and whites shows greater convergence when health is taken into account, as opposed to monetary income alone.

Therefore, in the case of black males, taking health into account suggests larger declines in disparity between blacks and whites than would be the case using income alone. Similarly, in the case of black females, we find the amount of income required to achieve full income parity with white females fell from a 22 percent increase in 1970 to an 12 percent increase in 2000, a decrease of eleven percentage points (50 percent relative decline).[5] By contrast, the difference in traditional incomes fell from 9 percent in 1970 to 4 percent in 2000, a decrease of five percentage points (55 percent relative decline). Compared to using traditional income alone, incorporating health into measures of well-being suggests a larger decline in black-white disparities in absolute terms and a roughly similar decline in relative terms.

In table 4-2, we present similar analyses focusing on lifetime income, which is simply the discounted expected value of the annual incomes shown in table 4-1. Put differently, lifetime income is computed by multiplying annual income by life expectancy, taking into account the fact that income earned in later years is worth less than income earned in earlier years due to discounting. As with annual income, we find greater convergence between blacks and whites when using lifetime full income rather than lifetime traditional income. In 1970, white males had larger lifetime traditional incomes than black males, due to both their higher annual incomes and their better health. Indeed, our results suggest that black males would have needed to have their lifetime incomes increased by 86 percent to attain traditional income parity with whites. By 2000, this figure fell to 62 percent, a decrease of 23 percentage points (28 percent relative decrease). When health is taken into account, we find that black males needed to have a 111 percent increase in lifetime income to achieve full lifetime income parity with whites in 1970 and a 76 percent increase in 2000, for a decrease of thirty-five percentage points overall (32 percent relative decrease). Similarly, for black females, traditional

TABLE 4-1

EVOLUTION OF BLACK-WHITE DISPARITIES
USING ANNUAL INCOME, 1970–2000

	Black income	White income	Traditional income disparity	WTA	Full income disparity
Males					
1970	$19,807	$34,690	75%	$21,916	111%
2000	$24,132	$37,726	56%	$18,363	76%
Change	*22%*	*9%*	*–19%*	*–16%*	*–35%*
Females					
1970	$7,889	$8,558	9%	$1,769	22%
2000	$17,529	$18,198	4%	$2,058	12%
Change	*122%*	*113%*	*–5%*	*16%*	*–11%*

SOURCE: Authors' calculations from the U.S. Current Population Survey (U.S. Census Bureau 2000). For details, see chapter 3.
NOTES: "Black income" and "white income" are average annual incomes for blacks and whites, respectively, calculated from the U.S. Current Population Survey. "Traditional income disparity" is the percentage increase in black income required to achieve income parity between blacks and whites. WTA is the absolute increase in black incomes required to attain parity in total well-being between the two groups, taking into account disparities in health. "Full income disparity" is the corresponding percentage increase. All dollar values are in 2008 dollars.

income disparity during this time period decreased from 14 percent to 6 percent (an absolute decrease of 8 percentage points and a relative decrease of 57 percent), while full income disparity fell from 22 percent to 12 percent (an absolute decrease of ten percentage points and a relative decrease of 45 percent).

Overall, then, our results suggest that incorporating health has two effects on black-white disparities. First, it increases the level of disparity in a given period because whites are healthier than blacks. It also suggests, however, a greater convergence than income measures alone show because black health has improved relative to white health over time. Put together, our results suggest that, although convergence in black-white earnings may be slowing, relative improvements in black health over time mean that convergence in black-white well-being may not be.

TABLE 4-2
EVOLUTION OF BLACK-WHITE DISPARITIES
USING LIFETIME INCOME, 1970–2000

	Black income	White income	Traditional income disparity	WTA	Full income disparity
			Males		
1970	$534,379	$991,784	86%	$591,281	111%
2000	$694,392	$1,126,672	62%	$528,381	76%
Change	30%	14%	−24%	−11%	−35%
			Females		
1970	$224,120	$254,801	14%	$50,266	22%
2000	$522,555	$556,386	6%	$61,361	12%
Change	133%	118%	−8%	22%	−10%

SOURCE: Authors' calculations from the U.S. Current Population Survey (U.S. Census Bureau 2000). For details, see chapter 3.
NOTES: "Black income" and "white income" are average lifetime incomes for blacks and whites, respectively, calculated from the U.S. Current Population Survey. "Traditional income disparity" is the percentage increase in black income required to achieve income parity between blacks and whites. WTA is the absolute increase in black incomes required to attain parity in total well-being between the two groups, taking into account disparities in health. "Full income disparity" is the corresponding percentage increase. All dollar values are in 2008 dollars.

Health and the Evolution of Economic Disparities across States

In the previous section, we examined how incorporating changes in health within races over time affected estimates of disparities in well-being between U.S. blacks and whites. In this section, we conduct a similar analysis of U.S. states. We first summarize the evolution of health and wealth disparities across states. We then ask how much greater would per-capita income have to be over time in the poorest U.S. state to achieve parity in income and total well-being (which accounts for income and the value of health) with the wealthiest U.S. state.

Evolution of Health Disparities across States. Our analysis begins by examining trends in health disparities across states. For white males in each

FIGURE 4-1

**1940–2000 GROWTH IN LIFE EXPECTANCY VERSUS
1940 LIFE EXPECTANCY, WHITE MALES**

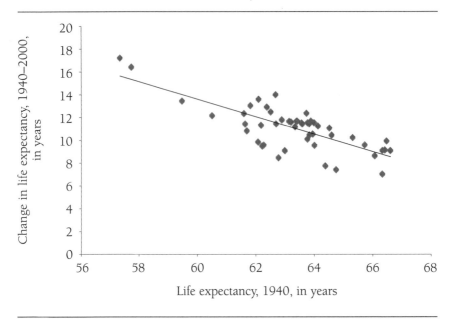

SOURCE: Authors' calculations based on data from the National Center for Health Statistics (Arias 2007).

state, figure 4-1 plots the growth in life expectancy between 1940 and 2000 against initial life expectancy in 1940. As discussed, published life tables for U.S. blacks do not exist from 1940, requiring us to focus our analysis of survival improvements in the earlier part of the twentieth century on whites alone. The data points in the figure clearly trend downward, indicating that states with higher white male life expectancy in 1940 experienced less growth in life expectancy between 1940 and 2000. Indeed, a simple regression procedure suggests that, on average, a 1.0 year increase in 1940 white male life expectancy was associated with a –0.78 year decrease in absolute life expectancy growth between 1940 and 2000. Put differently, if one were to consider two states, with state 1 having a life expectancy ten years higher than state 2 in 1940, our results imply that the average change in white male life expectancy would be 7.8 years *less* in state 1 than in state 2 with the lower life expectancy.

FIGURE 4-2

**1970–2000 GROWTH IN LIFE EXPECTANCY VERSUS
1970 LIFE EXPECTANCY, BLACK MALES**

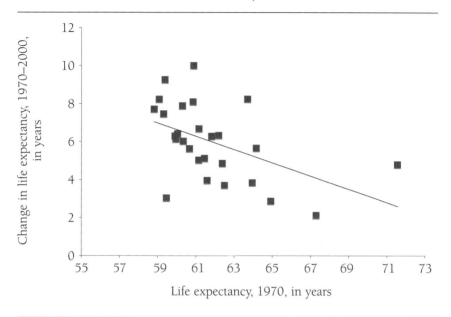

SOURCE: Authors' calculations based on data from the National Center for Health Statistics (Arias 2007).

In figure 4-2, we plot a similar graph for black males. Recall that for blacks, data on life expectancy by state is available only from 1970 onward, and for only twenty-seven states. As with whites, the plot is downward sloping, suggesting that states with higher life expectancy in 1970 experienced less absolute change between 1970 and 2000. Here again, a simple regression suggests that a 1.0 year increase in black male life expectancy in 1970 was associated with a –0.34 year decrease in absolute life expectancy growth between 1970 and 2000, so that a state with a black male life expectancy ten years higher than another in 1940 saw, on average, a 3.4 year decrease in life expectancy change between 1970 and 2000. Similar plots for females are shown in appendix 2 and show a similar conclusion. Across all demographic groups, then, life expectancy experienced higher growth in states with lower initial life expectancy.[6] Overall, these figures support convergence in life expectancy across states for each of the groups we consider.

Health and the Evolution of Income Growth across States. Having seen in figures 4-1 and 4-2, as well as in the associated figures in appendix 2, that life expectancy converged across states over time, we now examine the evolution of disparities in traditional income *and* full income, with the latter taking into account disparities in health *and* income across states. To illustrate, table 4-3 shows disparities in traditional income and full income for the five richest and poorest states in 1940 among white males. In both 1940 and 2000, the average traditional income among white males was the highest in the District of Columbia, rising from $15,822 to $45,627. In 1940, the next wealthiest state was New Jersey, which saw traditional incomes rise from $12,189 to $40,294 by 2000. Thus, compared to the District of Columbia, the additional income required for New Jersey to achieve traditional income parity fell from 29 percent to 14 percent, a 15 percentage point decrease. Incorporating the changes in life expectancy for both the District of Columbia and New Jersey from 1940 to 1970, our analysis shows that disparities in full income fell from 27 percent to 17 percent over this time period, a 10 percentage point decrease. In this case, the convergence in full income was actually *less* than the convergence in traditional income, suggesting that the value of health gains in the District of Columbia actually outpaced those in New Jersey.

Similarly, in 1940, the poorest state was Arkansas. Compared again to the District of Columbia, the average white male in Arkansas would have required a 303 percent increase in income to achieve traditional income parity in 1940. In 2000, however, white male residents of Arkansas required only a 112 percent increase in income to achieve traditional income parity, suggesting a significant amount of income convergence. Interestingly, because white males in Arkansas had similar life expectancies to white males in the District of Columbia in 1940, the additional income required to achieve full income parity was also 304 percent, identical to the amount required to achieve income parity in that year. In 2000, however, white males in Arkansas had lower life expectancies than those in the District of Columbia and therefore required an additional increase in income of 118 percent to achieve traditional income parity, compared to an additional 132 percent to achieve full income parity. Similar to the case of New Jersey, this again suggests that the value of health improvements in poorer states increased by relatively less compared to wealthier states.

TABLE 4-3
INCOME AND FULL INCOME DISPARITIES, SELECTED STATES, WHITE MALES, 1940–2000

State	1940		2000		1940–2000	
	Income	Traditional/ Full disparity	Income	Traditional/ Full disparity	Traditional reduction	Full reduction
District of Columbia	$15,822	0%/0%	$45,627	0%/0%	0%	0%
New Jersey	$12,189	29%/27%	$40,294	14%/17%	15%	10%
Connecticut	$11,246	39%/35%	$39,884	15%/17%	23%	18%
New York	$11,143	41%/39%	$32,580	41%/45%	0%	-5%
Massachusetts	$10,668	47%/45%	$34,567	33%/35%	14%	11%
Kentucky	$5,186	214%/230%	$23,113	103%/115%	111%	115%
Mississippi	$4,409	264%/274%	$24,143	95%/110%	169%	164%
South Dakota	$4,239	266%/252%	$20,312	126%/130%	139%	122%
North Dakota	$3,962	295%/287%	$20,703	122%/127%	173%	160%
Arkansas	$3,923	304%/304%	$21,500	118%/132%	186%	173%

SOURCE: Incomes obtained from Ruggles et al. (2008). Disparity calculations based on methods discussed in chapter 3.
NOTES: Traditional disparity is the income increase required to achieve income parity with the wealthiest per-capita income state in the given year (District of Columbia in 1940 and 2000), while full disparity is the income increase required to achieve parity in income per capita *and* health. "Traditional" and "full reduction" refer to 1940–2000 changes in traditional and full income disparities. All dollar values are 2008 dollars.

FIGURE 4-3

REDUCTIONS IN 1940–2000 INCOME AND FULL INCOME DISPARITIES
VERSUS 1940 INCOME, WHITE MALES

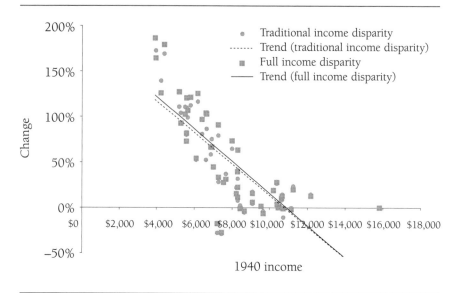

SOURCE: Incomes obtained from Ruggles et al. (2008). Traditional and full income disparities are calculated based on methods discussed in chapter 3.
NOTES: The graph plots 1940–2000 changes in traditional income disparity and full income disparity
as a function of 1940 per-capita income. Traditional income disparity is the income increase required
to achieve parity with the wealthiest per-capita income state in the given year (District of Columbia in
both 1940 and 2000), while full income disparity is the increase required to achieve parity in income
per capita *and* health. All dollar values are 2008 dollars.

Overall, table 4-3 presents two important findings. First, by increasing
their per-capita income more rapidly, white males in poorer states converged toward those in richer states from 1940 to 2000. Second, convergence in well-being between poor and wealthy states was vastly dominated
by reductions in traditional income disparities, as opposed to reductions in
health disparities. This is demonstrated by the last two columns of table 4-3,
which show convergence in traditional and full incomes to be roughly equal
for most states. In figure 4-3, we explore this further by graphing reductions
in income and full income disparities as a function of 1940 income for all
fifty states. The trends for both traditional and full income disparities are

TABLE 4-4
INCOME AND FULL INCOME DISPARITIES, SELECTED STATES, BLACK MALES, 1970–2000

State	1970		2000		1970–2000	
	Income	Traditional/ Full disparity	Income	Traditional/ Full disparity	Traditional reduction	Full reduction
Hawaii	$24,513	0%/0%	$21,339	15%/3%	-15%	-3%
Connecticut	$20,494	26%/41%	$21,678	18%/15%	9%	26%
Michigan	$20,314	30%/52%	$21,015	24%/28%	6%	24%
New Jersey	$18,994	36%/50%	$25,771	0%/0%	36%	50%
California	$18,730	35%/43%	$21,367	19%/17%	15%	26%
Louisiana	$9,652	174%/221%	$14,302	82%/87%	92%	134%
Alabama	$9,362	185%/241%	$13,946	87%/91%	99%	150%
South Carolina	$9,051	197%/261%	$14,902	74%/77%	123%	184%
Arkansas	$7,862	233%/283%	$13,771	89%/93%	144%	190%
Mississippi	$6,748	297%/376%	$11,827	120%/124%	177%	252%

SOURCE: Incomes obtained from Ruggles et al. (2008). Disparity calculations based on methods discussed in chapter 3.
NOTES: Traditional disparity is the income increase required to achieve income parity with the wealthiest per-capita income state in the given year (Hawaii in 1970 and New Jersey in 2000), while full disparity is the income increase required to achieve parity in income per capita and health. "Traditional" and "full reduction" refer to 1970–2000 changes in traditional and full disparities. All dollar values are 2008 dollars.

FIGURE 4-4

REDUCTIONS IN 1970–2000 INCOME AND FULL INCOME DISPARITIES VERSUS 1970 INCOME, BLACK MALES

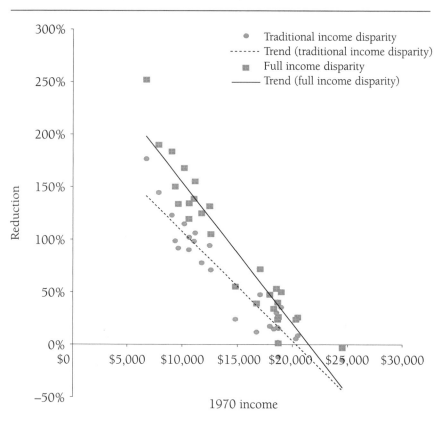

SOURCE: Incomes obtained from Ruggles et al. (2008). Traditional and full income disparities are cal-culated based on methods discussed in chapter 3.

NOTES: The graph plots 1970–2000 changes in traditional income disparity and full income disparity as a function of 1970 per-capita income. Traditional income disparity is the income increase required to achieve parity with the wealthiest per-capita income state in the given year (Hawaii in 1970 and New Jersey in 2000), while full income disparity is the increase required to achieve parity in income per capita *and* health. All dollar values are 2008 dollars.

downward sloping and nearly identical, confirming not only that poorer states in 1940 experienced larger relative increases in income and full income compared to wealthier states, but that these relative increases were driven mainly by relative gains in income alone.

Table 4-4 explores trends in income and full income disparities among black males, looking at the five richest and poorest states in 1970. Recall that for blacks, reliable data on income by state are available only from 1970 onward (and for only twenty-seven states), so our analysis focuses on changes between 1970 and 2000. Similar to white males, black males experienced convergence in income and full income across states over time, with poorer states experiencing larger reductions in income and full income disparities. In contrast to white males, however, as table 4-4 shows, reductions in full income disparities were generally larger than in traditional income disparities. Figure 4-4 demonstrates this point by graphing changes in income and full income disparities against 1970 incomes for all twenty-seven states. As with white males, both measures of disparity trend downward, showing that with both groups, poorer states in 1970 saw larger reductions in income and full income disparities. However, the trend for full income disparities is much steeper than the trend for traditional income disparities, suggesting that reductions in full income disparities exceeded reductions in traditional income disparities for poorer states. In appendix 2, we provide similar tables and figures for white and black females and find similar results.

Overall, then, our analysis demonstrates cross-state convergence in income and well-being for both whites and blacks, with poorer states experiencing larger reductions in income and full income disparities than richer states. For whites, reductions in full income disparities were driven almost exclusively by reductions in income disparities, suggesting that poorer states did not experience substantial gains in health relative to wealthier states. Meanwhile, for blacks, relative health improvements in poor compared to wealthy states played a large role in generating reductions in full income disparities over time. In this case, blacks in poor states enjoyed substantial relative improvements not only in income, but also in health. For blacks, convergence across states in traditional income understates convergence across states in well-being.

Conclusion

A vast literature has examined U.S. income disparities across races and states, and the conclusions are similar: although substantial reductions in economic disparities across races have occurred, they have generally slowed or even slightly reversed since the 1970s. Similarly, a large literature has examined disparities in health outcomes across races and suggests convergence in health disparities between blacks and whites since the 1970s. And while a number of studies have documented disparities in health across geographic regions, less effort has been made to examine the course of these disparities over time.

In merging these two strands of analyses, this present analysis had two objectives. The first was simply to review and summarize the evolution of wealth and health disparities across races and states. As shown in chapter 2, overall, we found substantial convergence in income and health between whites and blacks. Across states, however, we found that incomes actually diverged during our observation period. In the case of health disparities across states for whites, we found that disparity in life expectancy declined from 1940 to 1970 but increased slightly after that. We also found that these movements in health disparities were small in both relative and absolute terms and that they were also small relative to the decline in income disparity over this period. Compared to whites, however, blacks experienced much larger relative declines in health disparities across states between 1970 and 2000, although the absolute value of these declines was still small relative to the declines in income disparities over this time period.

With these results in hand, our second objective was to examine the extent to which trends in income disparities were affected by the value to individuals of reductions in health disparities. The central idea was that well-being is comprised not just of income, but of health as well. We found that, across races, full income disparities decreased more dramatically than income disparities, with the value of gains in health accounting for roughly the same reduction in inequality as changes in income. Thus, accounting for gains in health over time, our analysis suggests a greater move toward racial equality in well-being than would otherwise be predicted if income alone were used to measure well-being. For disparities in well-being across states, however, the picture is more mixed. For whites, accounting for health gains did not significantly affect gains in well-being for poorer states, but for blacks, accounting for health gains did imply larger improvements in equality between poorer and richer states.

There are several avenues for further work. First, our results suggest that disparities in health across races and states have been declining over time. Further work should try to clarify the causes of these decreases. In particular, given that substantial public funds are aimed at reducing disparities, it would be useful to measure the returns on public investments aimed at reducing health and income disparities. Such research could provide a targeted approach for policymakers interested in reducing economic disparities. Second, it is worthwhile to examine why disparities in health fell more for blacks across states, in relative terms, than for whites. Again, given that large sums are spent on reducing health disparities between blacks and whites, it would be interesting to examine whether an added effect of these expenditures was to reduce within-race differences across states. More generally, it is important to compare explicitly trends in within-race health disparities to trends in income disparities across races.

Overall, we believe our results suggest that accounting for health is an important component of any analysis of racial and geographic disparities in well-being. The point is not to downplay the lack of convergence in incomes, which is important and the subject of much research, but rather to suggest that alternative measures, such as full income, suggest a more optimistic view of trends in inequality. Because people value health in addition to income, we believe that full income is a better measure of the distribution of well-being across races and states and that incorporating health matters greatly.

Appendix 1
Derivation of Indirect Utility Functions

Theory

Our basic framework for valuing the improvements in survival for different states and racial groups is identical to the international analysis of Becker and others (2005), except now it is applied to a domestic context in which states (or racial groups) replace countries.[7] The main innovation of that analysis is a method of valuing large or inframarginal changes in survival. This extends earlier work by Usher (1973) and Murphy and Topel (2006), which values marginal changes in survival.

In particular, consider a hypothetical individual born in state i during year t—for example, Virginia in 1977. The lifetime indirect utility for this individual who faces lifetime income Y_{it} and cross-sectional survival $S_{it}(j)$ is given by:

$$V(Y, S) = \max \int_0^\infty e^{-\rho j} S_{it}(j) u(c_{it}(j)) dj \quad s.t.$$

$$\int_0^\infty e^{-\rho j} S_{it}(j) c_{it}(j) dj = \int_0^\infty e^{-\rho j} S_{it}(j) y_{it}(j) dj \quad (A.1)$$

where $S_{it}(j)$ is the survival function describing the probability of surviving j years (that is, to year $t + j$), $c_{it}(j)$ is consumption at year $t + j$, $y_{it}(j)$ is income in year $t + j$, ρ is the individual discount rate, and r is the interest rate. The budget constraint in this case assumes a perfect annuity market so that the discounted lifetime value of consumption equals the lifetime discounted value of earnings. When the market rate of discount equals the individual rate of discount and income $y_{it}(j)$ is assumed to be constant and equal to per-capita income in the year of birth, the above utility maximization yields the well-known condition that utility is maximized by having consumption equal to income in all periods, $c = y$.

The indirect utility above forms the basis for our valuation methodology. In particular, consider two entities (either separate states or racial groups) in the same time period. Each entity is assumed to face different annual (and therefore lifetime) incomes and survival prospects equivalent to the contemporaneous income and cross-sectional survival in that time period. Formally, incomes are represented by Y and Y', and survivals are represented by S and S'. The prime denotes, without loss of generality, the entity with higher lifetime income and better survival. In this framework, the amount of additional lifetime income WTA that would be required for individuals with lower income and survival Y and S to be equally well off as those with higher income and survival Y' and S' would be:

$$V(Y + WTA, S) = V(Y', S') \qquad (A.2)$$

This equality simply states that the lifetime indirect utility of those with low income and poor survival is equal to the lifetime indirect utility of those with high income and favorable survival when the poor are compensated by an amount equivalent to WTA. When states or races have identical survival prospects, this amount would trivially be equal to $WTA = Y' - Y$. To be equally well off as the rich, the poor would only need to be compensated by the difference between their income and the income of the rich. When the poor are also less healthy than the rich, so that $S < S'$, equality in economic well-being will require that the poor be additionally compensated by the economic value of the difference in survival.

To make this framework empirically tractable, we assume that annual income $y_{it}(j) = y$ is constant over time so that the lifetime income Y is given by:

$$Y = \int_0^\infty e^{-rj} S_{it}(j) y \, dj = A(S)y \qquad (A.3)$$

where $A(S)$ is the value of an annuity that pays one dollar each year, discounted by both the market rate of interest and the probability of survival S. Returning to our indirect utility equation (A.1), under the additional assumption that $r = \rho$, consumption equals income in all periods, so the indirect utility function can be written as

$$V(y, S) = u(y)A(S). \tag{A.4}$$

According to equation (A.4), the amount of additional annual income *wta* that would be required for individuals with lower annual income and survival y and S to be equally well off as those with higher income and survival y' and S' would be:

$$V(y + wta, S) = V(y', S'). \tag{A.5}$$

Note that the annual compensation required to leave both groups equally well off (*wta*) is related to the lifetime compensation required (*WTA*) according to: $WTA = wta \cdot A(S)$.

The valuation formula above (A.5) forms the empirical basis of our analysis of the evolution of economic inequality in the United States. Specifically, for each state and race, we can use estimated survival curves at birth to calculate the compensation required to make the poorest and unhealthiest race and states just as well off as their wealthier and healthier counterparts. Following the amount of compensation required over time gives an indication of how inequality in well-being measured by income alone (y) compares to inequality in well-being measured by both income and the value of improved health ($y + wta$).

Parameterizing the Model

To obtain a closed-form expression for *wta* that allows us to value improvements in survival with data on survival and income alone, we assume that instantaneous utility $u(c)$ takes on the following form:

$$u(c) = \frac{c^{1-1/\gamma}}{1 - 1/\gamma} + \alpha \tag{A.6}$$

where γ is the intertemporal elasticity of substitution and parameter α determines the level of consumption at which an individual would be indifferent between being alive or dead, in which case utility is normalized to zero. As noted by Becker and others (2005), this utility function captures two features that are important to understanding why improvements in mortality raise utility. First, improvements in survival in any given period allow consumption to be smoothed across all other periods, the value of which is determined by the intertemporal elasticity of substitution. Second, improvements in survival are more valuable the greater is the value of being alive relative to being dead, an aspect of our utility function captured by the parameter α. Based on the calibrations reported by Becker and others (2005), we set the intertemporal elasticity of substitution γ equal to 1.25, the normalization factor α to -14.97, and the annual interest rate to 3 percent. (For more details, we refer the interested reader to Becker et al. 2005.)

Under the maintained parameter assumptions, it is straightforward to show that wta satisfies:

$$wta = \left[\left(\frac{1}{1-\gamma} \right) \left(\frac{A(S')(y')^{1-1/\gamma}}{A(S)(1-1/\gamma)} - \alpha \right) \right]^{\frac{\gamma}{\gamma-1}} - y \qquad (A.7)$$

Equation (A.7) constitutes the empirical equation that allows us to calculate the value of improvements in survival.

Appendix 2
Additional Illustrations

Figures

Tables

FIGURE A2-1

**1940–2000 GROWTH IN LIFE EXPECTANCY VERSUS
1940 LIFE EXPECTANCY, WHITE FEMALES**

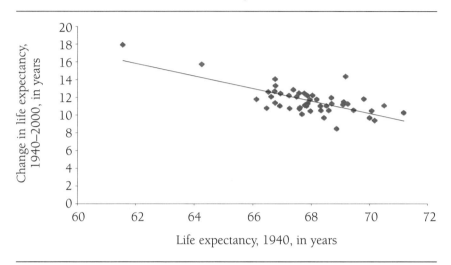

Life expectancy, 1940, in years

SOURCE: Life expectancy data obtained from the National Center for Health Statistics (Arias 2007).

FIGURE A2-2

**1970–2000 GROWTH IN LIFE EXPECTANCY VERSUS
1970 LIFE EXPECTANCY, BLACK FEMALES**

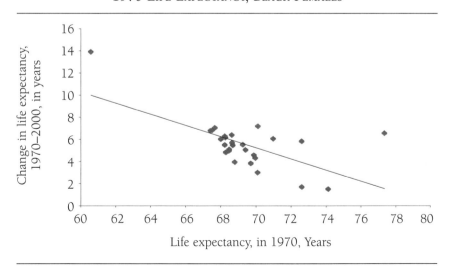

Life expectancy, in 1970, Years

SOURCE: Life expectancy data obtained from the National Center for Health Statistics (Arias 2007).

TABLE A2-1
INCOME AND FULL INCOME DISPARITIES, WHITE MALES, 1940–2000

State	1940		2000		1940–2000	
	Income	Traditional/ Full disparity	Income	Traditional/ Full disparity	Traditional reduction	Full reduction
District of Columbia	$15,822	0%/0%	$45,627	0%/0%	0%	0%
New Jersey	$12,189	29%/27%	$40,294	14%/17%	15%	10%
Connecticut	$11,246	39%/35%	$39,884	15%/17%	23%	18%
New York	$11,143	41%/39%	$32,580	41%/45%	0%	-5%
Massachusetts	$10,668	47%/45%	$34,567	33%/35%	14%	11%
California	$10,638	50%/52%	$32,523	42%/45%	8%	7%
Delaware	$10,462	50%/49%	$31,163	49%/55%	2%	-6%
Michigan	$10,404	52%/51%	$31,449	47%/51%	5%	0%
Nevada	$10,721	53%/62%	$28,537	63%/71%	-11%	-9%
Maryland	$10,390	53%/55%	$36,409	27%/29%	27%	25%
Illinois	$10,214	55%/54%	$34,272	35%/39%	20%	15%
Rhode Island	$9,667	62%/60%	$27,743	66%/69%	-4%	-10%
Ohio	$9,551	66%/65%	$28,319	64%/69%	2%	-4%
Washington	$9,084	73%/72%	$29,523	56%/59%	17%	13%
Pennsylvania	$9,084	75%/77%	$27,112	71%/77%	4%	0%
Wyoming	$8,655	84%/85%	$24,418	89%/94%	-5%	-9%
Oregon	$8,426	86%/82%	$25,153	83%/88%	2%	-6%
Indiana	$8,226	89%/82%	$27,882	67%/74%	22%	8%
New Hampshire	$8,285	90%/89%	$30,822	49%/51%	41%	37%
Utah	$8,301	91%/91%	$27,269	68%/71%	22%	20%
Florida	$8,297	93%/97%	$25,033	85%/92%	8%	5%
Virginia	$7,997	102%/111%	$33,523	38%/41%	65%	70%
Wisconsin	$7,676	103%/97%	$27,809	66%/69%	37%	28%

Arizona	$8,298	106%/137%	$26,672	74%/80%	32%	57%
Vermont	$7,550	110%/111%	$25,156	83%/87%	27%	24%
Montana	$7,445	113%/115%	$19,098	142%/150%	−29%	−35%
Maine	$7,283	120%/125%	$24,036	92%/97%	28%	29%
Minnesota	$6,930	123%/114%	$30,959	48%/49%	75%	65%
Colorado	$7,279	123%/135%	$31,906	44%/47%	79%	88%
West Virginia	$7,222	124%/135%	$18,609	152%/168%	−28%	−34%
Missouri	$7,017	126%/126%	$25,574	82%/89%	44%	37%
Louisiana	$6,883	134%/142%	$26,610	76%/85%	59%	57%
Texas	$6,661	146%/162%	$29,088	59%/65%	86%	97%
South Carolina	$6,417	155%/171%	$26,819	74%/83%	81%	88%
Idaho	$6,093	161%/162%	$22,124	108%/112%	52%	50%
Georgia	$6,183	161%/169%	$32,317	44%/50%	117%	119%
New Mexico	$6,623	163%/214%	$22,113	110%/119%	52%	95%
North Carolina	$5,792	178%/187%	$28,071	66%/72%	112%	114%
Iowa	$5,571	179%/169%	$23,512	96%/100%	83%	69%
Kansas	$5,500	183%/175%	$26,849	72%/78%	111%	97%
Tennessee	$5,642	185%/192%	$25,235	86%/97%	99%	95%
Oklahoma	$5,574	185%/186%	$22,898	105%/118%	80%	69%
Alabama	$5,576	189%/200%	$26,118	80%/91%	110%	109%
Nebraska	$5,271	194%/182%	$24,263	90%/94%	104%	89%
Kentucky	$5,186	214%/230%	$23,113	103%/115%	111%	115%
Mississippi	$4,409	264%/274%	$24,143	95%/110%	169%	164%
South Dakota	$4,239	266%/252%	$20,312	126%/130%	139%	122%
North Dakota	$3,962	295%/287%	$20,703	122%/127%	173%	160%
Arkansas	$3,923	304%/304%	$21,500	118%/132%	186%	173%

SOURCE: Incomes obtained from Ruggles et al. (2008). Disparity calculations based on methods discussed in chapter 3.

NOTES: Traditional disparity is the income increase required to achieve income parity with the wealthiest per-capita income state in the given year (District of Columbia in 1940 and 2000), while full disparity is the income increase required to achieve parity in income per capita *and* health. "Traditional" and "full reduction" refer to 1940–2000 changes in traditional and full income disparities. All dollar values are 2008 dollars.

TABLE A2-2
INCOME AND FULL INCOME DISPARITIES, BLACK MALES, 1970–2000

State	1970		2000		1970–2000	
	Income	Traditional/ Full disparity	Income	Traditional/ Full disparity	Traditional reduction	Full reduction
Hawaii	$24,513	0%/0%	$21,339	15%/3%	-15%	-3%
Connecticut	$20,494	26%/41%	$21,678	18%/15%	9%	26%
Michigan	$20,314	30%/52%	$21,015	24%/28%	6%	24%
New Jersey	$18,994	36%/50%	$25,771	0%/0%	36%	50%
California	$18,730	35%/43%	$21,367	19%/17%	15%	26%
District of Columbia	$18,723	42%/69%	$17,455	54%/68%	-12%	1%
Ohio	$18,669	41%/62%	$18,593	38%/38%	2%	24%
Illinois	$18,663	43%/71%	$20,604	27%/31%	16%	40%
Massachusetts	$18,544	40%/57%	$22,988	9%/4%	31%	53%
Indiana	$18,308	43%/64%	$20,225	28%/30%	15%	34%
New York	$17,949	48%/73%	$19,464	30%/26%	17%	48%
Maryland	$17,080	54%/79%	$24,223	7%/7%	48%	72%
Pennsylvania	$16,761	59%/90%	$17,682	47%/50%	12%	39%
Missouri	$14,819	80%/114%	$16,703	56%/59%	24%	55%
Texas	$12,589	109%/141%	$18,575	38%/36%	71%	105%
Virginia	$12,495	111%/147%	$21,813	17%/15%	94%	132%
Florida	$11,768	128%/174%	$17,116	50%/49%	78%	125%
Georgia	$11,186	140%/189%	$19,283	34%/34%	106%	155%

Kentucky	$11,082	138%/177%	$18,363	40%/38%	98%	139%
Tennessee	$10,640	147%/184%	$18,118	45%/50%	102%	134%
Oklahoma	$10,612	144%/172%	$16,735	54%/53%	90%	120%
North Carolina	$10,191	163%/218%	$17,430	49%/50%	115%	168%
Louisiana	$9,652	174%/221%	$14,302	82%/87%	92%	134%
Alabama	$9,362	185%/241%	$13,946	87%/91%	99%	150%
South Carolina	$9,051	197%/261%	$14,902	74%/77%	123%	184%
Arkansas	$7,862	233%/283%	$13,771	89%/93%	144%	190%
Mississippi	$6,748	297%/376%	$11,827	120%/124%	177%	252%

SOURCE: Incomes obtained from Ruggles et al. (2008). Disparity calculations based on methods discussed in chapter 3.

NOTES: Traditional disparity is the income increase required to achieve income parity with the wealthiest per-capita income state in the given year (Hawaii in 1970 and New Jersey in 2000), while full disparity is the income increase required to achieve parity in income per capita *and* health. "Traditional" and "full reduction" refer to 1970–2000 changes in traditional and full income disparities. All dollar values are 2008 dollars.

TABLE A2-3
INCOME AND FULL INCOME DISPARITIES, WHITE FEMALES, 1940–2000

State	1940		2000		1940–2000	
	Income	Traditional/ Full disparity	Income	Traditional/ Full disparity	Traditional reduction	Full reduction
District of Columbia	$6,616	0%/0%	$31,327	0%/0%	0%	0%
New York	$2,823	137%/140%	$16,705	90%/95%	47%	45%
Connecticut	$2,767	139%/139%	$19,099	66%/70%	73%	70%
New Jersey	$2,750	142%/145%	$18,027	76%/81%	66%	64%
Massachusetts	$2,696	147%/150%	$17,831	78%/82%	69%	68%
Rhode Island	$2,567	160%/162%	$14,147	124%/131%	35%	31%
California	$2,490	168%/172%	$16,485	93%/98%	76%	74%
Delaware	$2,364	183%/188%	$15,786	102%/111%	81%	77%
Maryland	$2,278	193%/198%	$18,707	70%/76%	123%	122%
Illinois	$2,198	203%/207%	$15,496	105%/112%	98%	95%
New Hampshire	$2,121	216%/222%	$15,096	110%/115%	106%	107%
Michigan	$1,838	264%/270%	$13,991	128%/136%	136%	134%
Ohio	$1,771	278%/285%	$13,492	137%/146%	142%	139%
Pennsylvania	$1,743	287%/297%	$12,946	146%/154%	141%	143%
Oregon	$1,674	294%/291%	$13,038	144%/152%	150%	140%
Florida	$1,701	294%/302%	$12,656	151%/158%	143%	144%
Nevada	$1,716	295%/308%	$15,945	101%/111%	194%	197%
Minnesota	$1,636	301%/295%	$16,449	92%/95%	209%	200%
Washington	$1,646	302%/301%	$14,530	118%/125%	183%	177%
North Carolina	$1,645	310%/322%	$14,079	127%/136%	183%	186%
Maine	$1,627	317%/333%	$12,534	154%/162%	163%	170%
South Carolina	$1,629	318%/337%	$12,808	149%/160%	169%	177%
Missouri	$1,600	320%/329%	$12,761	150%/161%	169%	168%

State						
Georgia	$1,595	323%/334%	$15,323	109%/118%	217%	214%
Virginia	$1,601	323%/339%	$16,791	89%/96%	243%	234%
Wisconsin	$1,561	325%/326%	$14,116	125%/130%	196%	200%
Arizona	$1,611	339%/383%	$13,403	137%/145%	238%	201%
Colorado	$1,545	343%/366%	$16,273	95%/101%	265%	248%
Wyoming	$1,510	344%/352%	$10,740	198%/211%	140%	146%
Utah	$1,471	351%/354%	$12,159	161%/168%	186%	191%
Montana	$1,482	353%/362%	$9,998	218%/229%	133%	135%
Vermont	$1,465	359%/371%	$13,462	137%/145%	226%	223%
Indiana	$1,445	364%/374%	$13,060	145%/156%	218%	219%
Iowa	$1,248	430%/429%	$12,700	150%/157%	272%	280%
Tennessee	$1,269	435%/455%	$12,259	162%/175%	280%	273%
Louisiana	$1,254	437%/452%	$11,040	190%/204%	248%	248%
West Virginia	$1,189	476%/504%	$9,347	244%/265%	239%	231%
Nebraska	$1,130	499%/519%	$12,988	144%/151%	368%	355%
Texas	$1,144	504%/543%	$13,666	133%/142%	401%	371%
New Mexico	$1,201	509%/605%	$11,639	174%/185%	420%	334%
Kansas	$1,073	516%/516%	$13,454	137%/145%	371%	380%
Alabama	$1,049	550%/577%	$11,540	177%/190%	387%	372%
Mississippi	$1,035	553%/574%	$11,037	191%/207%	367%	362%
Idaho	$1,019	556%/567%	$10,366	208%/219%	348%	349%
Oklahoma	$1,020	558%/572%	$11,331	184%/201%	371%	374%
Kentucky	$988	595%/634%	$11,172	187%/201%	432%	408%
North Dakota	$930	612%/614%	$10,889	190%/195%	419%	422%
South Dakota	$921	616%/612%	$11,370	178%/182%	430%	438%
Arkansas	$689	879%/905%	$10,286	212%/228%	678%	667%

SOURCE: Incomes obtained from Ruggles et al. (2008). Disparity calculations based on methods discussed in chapter 3.

NOTES: Traditional disparity is the income increase required to achieve income parity with the wealthiest per-capita income state in the given year (District of Columbia in 1940 and 2000), while full disparity is the income increase required to achieve parity in income per capita *and* health. "Traditional" and "full reductions" refer to 1940–2000 changes in traditional and full income disparities. All dollar values are 2008 dollars.

TABLE A2-4
INCOME AND FULL INCOME DISPARITIES, BLACK FEMALES, 1970–2000

State	1970		2000		1970–2000	
	Income	Traditional/ Full disparity	Income	Traditional/ Full disparity	Traditional reduction	Full reduction
District of Columbia	$12,175	0%/0%	$17,015	16%/19%	-16%	-19%
Hawaii	$9,774	18%/8%	$15,132	25%/18%	-6%	-9%
Connecticut	$9,403	28%/26%	$15,338	25%/23%	3%	3%
New York	$8,912	36%/35%	$14,098	36%/33%	0%	1%
New Jersey	$8,708	49%/65%	$17,352	12%/13%	36%	52%
Maryland	$8,423	44%/43%	$19,422	0%/0%	44%	43%
California	$8,361	41%/34%	$13,188	47%/45%	-5%	-11%
Illinois	$8,300	47%/49%	$14,744	33%/36%	14%	13%
Indiana	$7,787	56%/55%	$14,560	34%/34%	22%	21%
Michigan	$7,528	61%/61%	$14,135	39%/41%	23%	20%
Massachusetts	$7,448	60%/55%	$15,172	26%/22%	34%	33%
Pennsylvania	$7,171	70%/71%	$13,159	48%/49%	22%	22%
Ohio	$7,127	70%/68%	$13,300	46%/47%	23%	21%
Missouri	$6,781	80%/81%	$13,088	49%/50%	31%	31%
Florida	$5,537	123%/127%	$12,476	56%/57%	66%	70%
Texas	$5,474	122%/121%	$11,750	65%/65%	56%	55%
Virginia	$5,254	132%/133%	$14,870	30%/29%	102%	103%
North Carolina	$5,229	135%/138%	$12,442	57%/58%	78%	80%

Kentucky	$5,163	137%/138%	$11,695	67%/68%	70%	71%
Tennessee	$5,010	144%/146%	$13,282	48%/51%	96%	95%
Oklahoma	$4,914	143%/135%	$10,063	93%/94%	50%	41%
Georgia	$4,847	154%/159%	$13,829	41%/41%	113%	118%
South Carolina	$4,217	192%/197%	$10,688	82%/84%	109%	114%
Louisiana	$3,680	232%/234%	$9,119	115%/118%	117%	116%
Alabama	$3,328	269%/275%	$10,103	93%/95%	176%	180%
Arkansas	$3,052	297%/295%	$9,440	108%/112%	190%	183%
Mississippi	$2,958	316%/324%	$9,144	115%/119%	202%	205%

SOURCE: Incomes obtained from Ruggles et al. (2008). Disparity calculations based on methods discussed in chapter 3.

NOTES: Traditional disparity is the income increase required to achieve income parity with the wealthiest per-capita income state in the given year (District of Columbia in 1970 and Maryland in 2000), while full disparity is the income increase required to achieve parity in income per capita *and* health. "Traditional" and "full reductions" refer to 1970–2000 changes in traditional and full income disparities. All dollar values are 2008 dollars.

FIGURE A2-3

**REDUCTIONS IN 1940–2000 INCOME AND FULL INCOME DISPARITIES
VERSUS 1940 INCOME, WHITE FEMALES**

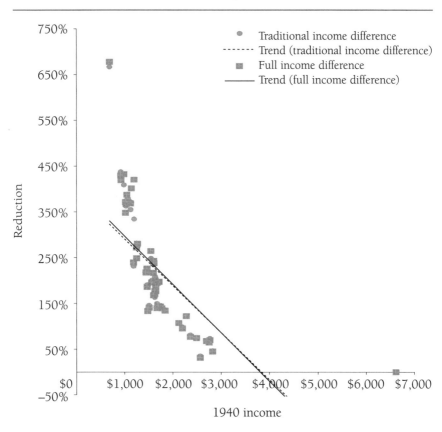

SOURCE: Incomes obtained from Ruggles et al. (2008). Traditional and full income disparities are calculated based on methods discussed in chapter 3.

NOTES: The graph plots 1940–2000 changes in traditional income disparity and full income disparity as a function of 1940 per-capita income. Traditional income disparity is the income increase required to achieve parity with the wealthiest per-capita income state in the given year (District of Columbia in 1940 and 2000), while full income disparity is the income increase required to achieve parity in income per capita *and* health. All dollar values are 2008 dollars.

Figure A2-4

Reductions in 1970–2000 Income and Full Income Disparities versus 1970 Income, Black Females

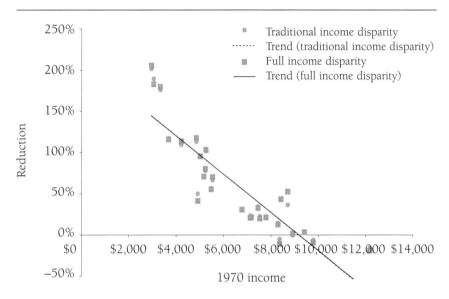

Source: Incomes obtained from Ruggles et al. (2008). Traditional and full income disparities are calculated based on methods discussed in chapter 3.

Notes: The graph plots 1970–2000 changes in traditional income disparity and full income disparity as a function of 1970 per-capita income. Traditional income disparity is the income increase required to achieve parity with the wealthiest per-capita income state in the given year (District of Columbia in 1970 and Maryland in 2000), while full income disparity is the income increase required to achieve parity in income per capita *and* health. All dollar values are 2008 dollars.

Notes

1. As noted in Neal (2006), one drawback of using the Current Population Survey to measure black-white income differences is that the CPS does not sample the prison population. Given the large increase in the number of black inmates since the 1970s, our results will understate the difference in black-white earnings since the 1970s if inmates have lower earnings than non-inmates. This effect is likely to be small, however, as 3.5 percent of black males and 0.2 percent of black females were imprisoned in 2000 (U.S. Department of Justice, Bureau of Justice Statistics 2001).

2. Published state-specific life tables for blacks did not exist in 1940 and existed for only twenty-six states in 1970; see chapter 3.

3. Conversely, if the wealthier group is less healthy ($S' < S$), then equation (1) implies that *WTA* will be less than the difference in income. In this case, the better health of the poorer group offsets its lower income.

4. For the probability of dying at ages greater than eight-five, we used the method for life table extrapolation detailed by the National Center for Health Statistics (Arias 2007).

5. Intriguingly, table 4-1 shows that the absolute amount required to achieve parity in well-being between white and black females actually rose from $1,769 in 1970 to $2,058 in 2000. As discussed in chapter 2, this increase is due to the large income increases experienced by both groups between 1970 and 2000. Thus, the relevant measure is the amount required to achieve well-being as a share of black income.

6. For white and black females, see figures A2-1 and A2-2 in appendix 2.

7. This framework is also used to value improvements in U.S. HIV/AIDS survival by Jena and Philipson (2008).

References

Altonji, J. G., and R. M. Blank. 1999. Race and Gender in the Labor Market. In *Handbook of Labor Economics,* ed. O. Ashenfelter and D. Card. Amsterdam, Netherlands: Elsevier.

———, and C. R. Pierret. 2001. Employer Learning and Statistical Discrimination. *Quarterly Journal of Economics* 116 (1): 313–50.

Arias, E. 2007. United States Life Tables, 2004. *National Vital Statistics Reports* 56 (9): 1–40.

Atkinson, A. 1970. On the Measurement of Inequality. *Journal of Economic Theory* 2 (3): 244–63.

Ayanian, J. Z., P. D. Cleary, J. S. Weissman, and A. M. Epstein. 1999. The Effect of Patients' Preferences on Racial Differences in Access to Renal Transplantation. *New England Journal of Medicine* 341 (22): 1661–69.

Baicker, K., A. Chandra, and J. S. Skinner. 2005. Geographic Variation in Health Care and the Problem of Measuring Racial Disparities. *Perspectives in Biology and Medicine* 48 (Suppl.): S42–S53.

Barnato, A. E., F. L. Lucas, D. Staiger, D. E. Wennberg, and A. Chandra. 2005. Hospital-Level Racial Disparities in Acute Myocardial Infarction Treatment and Outcomes. *Medical Care* 43 (4): 308–19.

Barro, R., and X. Sala-i-Martin. 1991. Convergence across States and Regions. *Brookings Papers on Economic Activity* 1:107–58.

———. 1992. Convergence. *Journal of Political Economy* 100 (2): 223–51.

———. 1995. *Economic Growth.* Advanced Series in Economics. New York: McGraw-Hill.

Beck, A. J. and P. M. Harrison. 2001. Prisoners in 2000. U.S. Department of Justice. Bureau of Justice Statistics. *Bureau of Justice Statistics Bulletin.* NCJ 188207. August.

Becker, G., T. Philipson, and R. Soares. 2005. The Quantity and Quality of Life and the Evolution of World Inequality. *American Economic Review* 95 (1): 277–91.

Bernard, A., and C. Jones. 1996. Productivity and Convergence across U.S. States and Industries, *Empirical Economics* 21 (1): 113–35.

Bernat, A. 2001. Convergence in State Personal Income: 1950–1999. *Survey of Current Business* 81:36–48.

Breslin, T. M., A. M. Morris, N. Gu, S. L. Wong, E. V. Finlayson, M. Banerjee, and J. D. Birkmeyer. 2009. Hospital Factors and Racial Disparities in Mortality after Surgery for Breast and Colon Cancer. *Journal of Clinical Oncology* 27 (24): 3945–50.

Brown, C. P., L. Ross, I. Lopez, A. Thornton, and G. E. Kiros. 2008. Disparities in the Receipt of Cardiac Revascularization Procedures between Blacks and Whites: An Analysis of Secular Trends. *Ethnicity and Disease* 18 (2 Suppl. 2): S2-112–17.

Chandra, A., and J. S. Skinner. 2004. Geography and Racial Health Disparities. In *Critical Perspectives on Racial and Ethnic Differences in Health in Late Life,* ed. N. B. Anderson, R. A. Bulatao, and B. Cohen. Washington, DC: National Academies Press.

Crain, W. M. 2003. *Volatile States: Institutions, Policy, and the Performance of American State Economies.* Ann Arbor: University of Michigan Press.

Deaton, A. 2003. Health, Inequality, and Economic Development. *Journal of Economic Literature* 41 (1): 113–58.

De la Fuente, Angel. 1997. The Empirics of Growth and Convergence: A Selective Review. *Journal of Economic Dynamics and Control* 21 (1): 23–73.

Fowler, F. J., P. M. Gallagher, D. L. Anthony, K. Larsen, and J. S. Skinner. 2008. Relationship between Per Capita Medicare Expenditures and Patient Perceptions of Quality of Care. *JAMA* 299 (20): 2406–12.

Giles, W. H., R. F. Anda, M. L. Casper, L. G. Escobedo, H. A. Taylor. 1995. Race and Sex Differences in Rates of Invasive Cardiac Procedures in U.S. Hospitals. Data from the National Hospital Discharge Survey. *Archives of Internal Medicine* 155 (3): 318–24.

Gottschalk, P. 1997. Inequality, Income Growth and Mobility: The Basic Facts. *Journal of Economic Perspectives* 11 (2): 21–40.

Hannan, E. L., M. van Ryn, J. Burke, D. Stone, D. Kumar, D. Arani, W. Pierce, S. Rafii, T. A. Sanborn, S. Sharma, J. Slater, and B. A. DeBuono. 1999. Access to Coronary Artery Bypass Surgery by Race/Ethnicity and Gender among Patients Who Are Appropriate for Surgery. *Medical Care* 37 (1): 68–77.

Herholz, H., D. C. Goff, D. J. Ramsey, F. A. Chan, C. Ortiz, D. Labarthe, and L. Z. Nichaman. 1996. Women and Mexican Americans Receive Fewer Cardiovascular Drugs Following Myocardial Infarction than Men and Non-Hispanic Whites: The Corpus Christi Heart Project, 1988–1990. *Journal of Clinical Epidemiology* 49 (3): 279–87.

Institute of Medicine. 2003. *Unequal Treatments: Confronting Racial and Ethnic Disparities in Health Care.* Washington, DC: National Academies Press.

Jena, A. B., and T. Philipson. 2008. *Innovation and Technology Adoption in Health Care Markets.* Washington, DC: AEI Press.

Juhn, C., K. M. Murphy, B. Pierce. 1991. Accounting for the Slowdown in Black-White Wage Convergence. In *Workers and Their Wages: Changing Patterns in the United States,* ed. Marvin Kosters, 107–43. Washington, DC: AEI Press.

Kaplan, G. A., E. R. Pamuk, J. W. Lynch, R. D. Cohen, and J. L. Balfour. 1996. Inequality in Income and Mortality in the United States: Analysis of Mortality and Potential Pathways. *British Medical Journal* 312 (7037): 999–1003.

Kim, S. 1998. Economic Integration and Convergence: U.S. Regions, 1840–1987. *Journal of Economic History* 58 (3): 659–83.

Kressin, N. R., and L. A. Petersen. 2001. Racial Differences in the Use of Invasive Cardiovascular Procedures: Review of the Literature and Prescription for Future Research. *Annals of Internal Medicine* 135 (5): 352–66.

Levy, F. 2008. Distribution of Income. In *Concise Encyclopedia of Economics,* ed. D. R. Henderson. Indianapolis: Library of Economics and Liberty. http://www.econlib.org/library/Enc/DistributionofIncome.html (accessed January 15, 2010).

Lucas, R. 1988. On the Mechanics of Development Planning. *Journal of Monetary Economics* 22 (1): 342.

Lynch, J. W., G. A. Kaplan, E. R. Pamuk, R. D. Cohen, K. E. Heck, J. L. Balfour, and I. H. Yen. 1998. Income Inequality and Mortality in Metropolitan Areas of the United States. *American Journal of Public Health* 88 (7): 1074–80.

Mankiw, N. G., D. Romer, and D. N. Weil. 1992. A Contribution to the Empirics of Economic Growth. *Quarterly Journal of Economics* 107 (2): 407–37.

Marmot, M. 1999. Multilevel Approaches to Understanding Social Determinants. In *Social Epidemiology,* ed. L. Berkman and I. Kawachi, 349–67. Oxford: Oxford University Press.

———, S. Stansfeld, C. Patel, F. North, J. Head, I. White, E. Brunner, A. Feeney, G. D. Smith. 1991. Health Inequalities among British Civil Servants: The Whitehall II Study. *Lancet* 337 (8754): 1387–93.

Maxwell, N. 1994. The Effect on Black-White Wage Differences of Differences in the Quantity and Quality of Education. *Industrial and Labor Relations Review* 47 (2): 249–64.

Murphy, K., and R. Topel. 2006. Value of Health and Longevity. *Journal of Political Economy* 114 (5): 871–904.

Neal, D. A. 2006. Why Has the Black-White Skill Convergence Stopped? In *Handbook of the Economics of Education,* ed. E. Hanushek and F. Welch, 511–76. Amsterdam, Netherlands: Elsevier.

———, and W. R. Johnson. 1996. The Role of Premarket Factors in Black-White Wage Differences. *Journal of Political Economy* 104 (5): 869–95.

O'Neill, J. 1990. The Role of Human Capital in Earnings Differences between Black and White Men. *Journal of Economic Perspectives* 4 (4): 25–45.

Parente, S. L., and E. C. Prescott. 1993. Changes in the Wealth of Nations. *Federal Reserve Bank of Minneapolis Quarterly Review* 17 (2): 3–16.

Peek, M. E., A. Cargill, and E. S. Huang. 2007. Diabetes Health Disparities: A Systematic Review of Health Care Interventions. *Medical Care Research and Review* 64 (5 Suppl.): 101S–56S.

Peltzman, S. 2009a. Mortality Inequality. George J. Stigler Center for the Study of the Economy and the State Working Paper 225, Booth School of Business, University of Chicago.

————. 2009b. Mortality Inequality. *Journal of Economic Perspectives* 23 (4): 175–90.

Quah, D. T. 1996. Empirics for Economic Growth and Convergence. *European Economic Review* 40 (6): 1353–75.

Romer, P. 1986. Increasing Returns and Long-Run Growth. *Journal of Political Economy* 94 (5): 1002–37.

Ruggles, S., M. Sobek, T. Alexander, C. A. Fitch, R. Goeken, P. K. Hall, M. King, and C. Ronnander. 2008. Integrated Public Use Microdata Series: Version 4.0. Machine-readable database. Minneapolis, MN: Minnesota Population Center.

Skinner, J., and W. Zhou. 2006. The Measurement and Evolution of Health Inequality: Evidence from the U.S. Medicare Population. In *Public Policy and Income Distribution*, ed. A. J. Auerbach, D. Card, and J. M. Quigley. New York: Russell Sage Foundation.

Smith, J. 1999. Healthy Bodies and Thick Wallets. *Journal of Economic Perspectives* 13 (2): 145–66.

————. 2007. The Impact of Socioeconomic Status over the Life-Course. *Journal of Human Resources* 42 (4): 739–64.

Terplan, M., E. J. Smith, and S. M. Temkin. 2009. Race in Ovarian Cancer Treatment and Survival: A Systematic Review with Meta-Analysis. *Cancer Causes and Control* 20:1139–50.

Turner, M. A., M. Fix, and R. Struyk. 1991. *Opportunities Denied, Opportunities Diminished: Racial Discrimination in Hiring.* Report 91-9. Washington, DC: Urban Institute Press.

U.S. Census Bureau. 2000. *Current Population Survey: Basic Monthly Data, 1977–2000.* Washington, DC: U.S. Department of Commerce, Bureau of the Census (producer); Cambridge, MA: National Bureau of Economic Research (distributor).

Usher, D. 1973. An Imputation to the Measure of Economic Growth for Changes in Life Expectancy. In *The Measurement of Economic and Social Performance, Studies in Income and Wealth* 38, ed. M. Milton, 193–225. New York: Columbia University Press.

Vigdor, J. 2006. The New Promised Land: Black-White Convergence in the American South, 1960–2000. NBER Working Paper No. 12143.

About the Authors

Anupam B. Jena, MD, PhD, is a medical resident in the Department of Internal Medicine, Massachusetts General Hospital, Harvard Medical School. He is also a visiting fellow at the Bing Center for Health Economics at the RAND Corporation. Dr. Jena's research focuses on the economic value of medical innovation, the implications of cost-effectiveness policies for technological growth, and the economics of global public health. His work has been published in journals including *Annals of Internal Medicine, Health Affairs, Health Economics, Health Services Research, Journal of Law and Economics, American Journal of Managed Care, BE Press Forum for Health Economics and Policy,* and *Journal of Health Economics.* In 2007, he received the Eugene Garfield Award from Research!America for a paper coauthored with Tomas J. Philipson on the economic impact of medical technology. A member of Phi Beta Kappa, Dr. Jena earned his undergraduate degrees in economics and biology from the Massachusetts Institute of Technology. He received his MD from the Pritzker School of Medicine at the University of Chicago and his PhD from the university's Department of Economics.

Tomas J. Philipson, PhD, is the Daniel Levin Professor of Public Policy Studies at the Irving B. Harris Graduate School of Public Policy Studies at the University of Chicago. Dr. Philipson was a health care adviser to the presidential campaign of John McCain in 2008 and served as senior economic adviser to the head of the U.S. Food and Drug Administration from 2003 to 2004 and as senior economic adviser to the head of the Centers for Medicare and Medicaid Services from 2004 to 2005. Dr. Philipson is the recipient of numerous international and national research awards and was awarded the highest honor in his field, the prestigious Kenneth Arrow Award of the International Health Economics Association, in 2000 and

2006. He obtained his undergraduate degree in mathematics at Uppsala University, Sweden, and received his MA and PhD in economics from the Wharton School and the University of Pennsylvania.

Eric Sun, MD, PhD, is a resident in the Department of Anesthesiology at Stanford University and a visiting fellow at the Bing Center for Health Economics at the RAND Corporation. His research has examined the costs and benefits of medical R&D, the role of the FDA and product liability in ensuring drug safety, and the economics of global public health. Dr. Sun's work has been published in the *Journal of Health Economics, American Journal of Managed Care, Journal of Public Economics, Health Affairs, Health Economics, Health Services Research,* and *BE Press Forum for Health Economics and Policy.* Dr. Sun graduated from Princeton University with an AB in molecular biology, from the Pritzker School of Medicine at the University of Chicago with an MD, and from the Booth School of Business with a PhD in business economics.